ALSO BY WALLIS WILDE-MENOZZI

Mother Tongue: An American Life in Italy

Toscanelli's Ray

The Other Side
of the Tiber

The Other Side of the Tiber

Reflections on Time in Italy

WALLIS WILDE-MENOZZI

Farrar, Straus and Giroux

New York

Farrar, Straus and Giroux
18 West 18th Street, New York 10011

Owing to limitations of space, illustration credits can be
found on pages 365–69, and acknowledgments for permission
to reprint previously published material can be found on pages 371–72.

Library of Congress Cataloging-in-Publication Data
Wilde-Menozzi, Wallis.
The other side of the Tiber : reflections on time in Italy /
Wallis Wilde-Menozzi. — 1st ed.
    p. cm.
ISBN 978-0-374-53431-8 (hardcover)
    1. Italy—Social life and customs.   2. Italy—Description and travel.
3. Wilde-Menozzi, Wallis—Travel—Italy.   4. Wilde-Menozzi, Wallis—
Homes and haunts—Italy.   I. Title.

GT2402.I8 W55 2013
945.092—dc23
                                                        2012034571

Designed by Jonathan D. Lippincott

www.fsgbooks.com
www.twitter.com/fsgbooks • www.facebook.com/fsgbooks

P1

To Beatrice, who, at two,
already loves fountains, statues, and good bread

The straight line cannot proceed through the torturous twists of life.
—Giambattista Vico, Italian philosopher (1668–1744)

CONTENTS

I

Memory

The poet seeks what is nowhere in all the world and yet somewhere
[s]he finds it.

—Plautus, circa 180 B.C.E.

1

"*Tevere*," he said. I was in a truck heading to Rome, hitching a ride. But when I reconstruct the conversation, when the truck driver continued to shout, "*Tevere, Tevere,*" as he gestured beyond the autostrada, I can't find many details. I was on my first trip to Italy, a student in a miniskirt and with little sense of danger. I was not yet teaching in Oxford.

That he was talking about the river Tiber, flowing down to the sea at Ostia, below the Po, below the Arno, the old river that is older than the Latins and more forcefully managed than all the Roman legions, never crossed my mind. Nothing I knew corresponded to those syllables and I could not fit them to the small cars, the Cinquecentos, and shaggy eucalyptus trees along the shoulders of the road. I was stumped and embarrassed.

I had gotten that far hitching from Oslo and briefly crossing into East Berlin.

The word the truck driver was shouting was far enough from the sounds in English that I couldn't make the leap. Why that moment in particular has remained a vivid memory, I can't say, except that it holds something that squirms with life. The recollection physically stirs my stomach: It's not all pleasant nor all bad, nor the only time that the perception of hurling forward without knowing enough has coincided with a feeling that an insignificant event is hinting at something greater.

The sensation of frustration exists, pristine, suspended from the exact moment I could not see the broad, often muddy river that must have been flitting in and out of view. Some memories are seeds, randomly dropped, but they hold their inheritances intact, waiting to spring from the right ground. We notice them when they unexpectedly bloom.

2

Four years later I came to know the real Tiber after I impetuously fled to the Eternal City, leaving a tenured job and my first marriage, which was troubled from the beginning. I chose Rome because it seemed an easy place to survive. I left Oxford overnight, hurt, angry, and frighteningly free, carrying my portable Smith-Corona and fifty pounds sterling. With that dramatic break, I started to refind independence and unbury my wish to become a writer. I stayed, living alone near the Campo de' Fiori in 1968, 1969, and part of 1970. Later I came back to Italy, later still married an Italian, and have now lived in Parma for thirty years. The Tiber in Rome is most vivid to me as a thick brown flow lined by synchronized rowers in the spring and a steelier, stronger force shadowed by gulls in November. Most summer days toward evening, it becomes hammered sheets of copper and gold. When currents slow, its waves polish themselves into swirling columns of marble.

The Tiber is where these reflections begin. The long dialogue with Italy started with a word, *Tevere*, a name that I could not see and did not know. It started because I was looking for something fundamental. Often, like the impenetrable word, the real world seemed as if it were running parallel, hidden to me. A few basics in that dialogue are clear to me now. Many exchanges took place without my making conscious choices. Most let me explore what holds life together.

Italy possesses extraordinary master keys that it offers to everyone, even without their asking. It takes time to discover which ones work. Many that I tried opened strong and stunning realities

beyond my shadow's reach. Many led me, as they have so many others, to learn more about the heart.

3

It would not be necessary to point out my salt-and-pepper hair in order to reveal that I am no longer the same person as the girl hitching a ride. Nor do we need to dwell on disturbing spectacles of Italy's recent leader for conclusive evidence that the Italy of modest lifestyles, the Cinquecentos, the small cars and safe rides that once existed, no longer is the norm. I think, though, if I observe, as Heraclitus did, that the river is never the same, any changes I describe will be deduced from looking at surfaces and totaling up statistics.

Instead, I want to focus on the slow moves of the self: its transformations, however sputtering and unwilled. There, change appears more circular and takes us in more meditative directions. This is the experience I wish to give words to. I want to frame the effect of time carrying earlier time in Italy and how this shapes perception. This version of time happens, in part, because Bernini's angels and Virgil's *Bucolics* continue to exist and claim attention. Paleolithic peoples' flint blades found in the mountains carry traces of having cut grain and meat; it makes yesterday seem a very long stretch. Prayers carved in Ligurian seawalls still cry out into the darkness of today's violent seas. My point of view dwells on depths too deep for projection; physical presences too numerous to initiate discussion without acknowledging dense, tangled, and endlessly defined human roots. Even if one has the radio on and it is tuned to the present, a battered bell from some ancient tower will still count the hour.

Sfogliatelle, the shell-shaped pastries filled with ricotta, are nearly the same today as when I first bit into their crispy layers on a street in Rome so long ago. Probably the pastry remains a quite good attempt at replicating the sweet that was made when Neapolitans rolled out their sheets of dough in the seventeenth century. The sweet is a conscious effort to deny time its novelty. It must be done in a certain way. It speaks of a certain place, of certain people: a mother and a grandmother. That particular connotation of abundance, piccolo tastes of pleasure and long gazes of time and repetition, draws on a sense that certain things, if not eternal, have reason to be perpetual. The layers of significance are the result of a particularly Italian mentality that has been cultivated, often at a great price. To those who inherit the mentality, it is a basic spell, too enchanting and old to imagine why one would ever want to give it up. Memory as time that stays never allows for a freely running river, and thus life cannot be seen that way.

When you get into an Italian river, the story is not that you cannot step into the same river twice. You know you will, even when you wish to assert that you are free of all that. You step in, recognizing that you are surrounded, as so many generations have been. Some Cassandra may warn you to look out for sharks. This will seem an absurd intrusion, another instance of myth. But the observer will insist that it's important to keep your eyes skeptically scanning. Then he will mention evil. It's annoying to worry about evil on a beautiful day amid such extraordinary beauty. But he will hold his ground, because Italians have tenacious memories. If a shark happens to appear, he warns, more will gather. This most probably nonexistent shark, this darkness, slithers deep, even when clear water is showing only blue sky.

II

Private Lessons

Should I use Gianni Agnelli or Queen Elizabeth as a reference?
—Italian student of English

1

The Tiber in all seasons carried the city. It offered the centerpiece for nature in a city shaped and colored by hills, flowering plants, and scented trees. Its movement, rolling or snaking smoothly, was the heart I touched, since it was only a few blocks from the courtyard in which I occupied two small rooms on two floors. To reach the river, I cut past the massive and wonderfully rational Farnese Palace and then turned left, following a path where I could eventually see the Isola Tiberina, or right, where the angels planned by Bernini on the Ponte Sant'Angelo gave a horizontal and vertical torque to its crenellated movement underneath. The fact that in those few minutes I had just passed a Renaissance palace designed by Sangallo and Michelangelo, enhanced by two vast granite tubs in the piazza from the Baths of Caracalla, where ancient Romans once soaked, and then could either pass the synagogue, a relatively new building on the edge of the two overlapping Jewish quarters, one dating from the time of Christ and the other from the 1500s, when Sephardic Jews were expelled from Spain, or cross over toward the Castel Sant'Angelo and the sprall of the Vatican, made any errand in the city, along the Tiber or, in other directions, toward Piazza Navona or Piazza Venezia, where Mussolini pronounced his demagogic speeches, into an event that invariably collected unexpected satisfactions.

2

Any walk involves a lot of taking in. It's a two-way dynamic here because Rome always offers a reciprocal invitation. You, too, belong to its landscape. Rome plunges you into a continuous attitude of attention, not only because of its unruly traffic but also because its layers lift thought and feeling beyond basic concerns. Getting bread or a fiasco of Frascati? You have just passed the columns where Brutus assassinated Caesar. As it has for centuries, Rome's particular physiognomy offers history as presence more than burden. Muttering like a senile relative or seducing like a mysterious veiled figure, it reaches out and includes you in its clamor and predicament. Each day you notice that you breathe in a different way. In front of unbearable beauty, you gasp. Facing signs of history's ferocious cruelties, that same startled breath, with different pain, issues from inside.

This mantle of emotions wrapped me up. Every day instead of abandoning me to my lack of certainty, the city offered inclusion. It negated the fantasy of being an alienated speck or another heartbroken woman headed for psychosomatic illness or, worse, suicide. As steadily as the wide Tiber, Rome eased me into the

mystery of life. My little coal-burning stove and the new feature of running water in my two rooms added connections that simplified my needs. My craving for life beyond myself, from the amphitheater of my courtyard, where I heard human voices day and night, to Bernini's semicircular arcades, with their eye-blinding whir of columns to gather the populace standing in front of Saint Peter's, was satisfied by the uncontainable book of human drama that always seemed to be read out loud in Rome.

It is difficult to feel left out in a city with so many extravagant fountains and steep steps. When barefoot beggars, some bright-eyed, some crippled and defeated, hunch in dark corners and plead, you are strangely tempered by how many face bad luck. The soaring curves of hundreds of churches, with indentations on doors and basins rubbed smooth by hands searching for hope, add to a dense physical consciousness that begins to take hold. All of the layers, finished and unfinished, push one toward a sense of irony and wonder that humanity has made so many moves and is still undeterred. Streams of foreigners with open guidebooks wander through the streets on inspired and dedicated journeys. Every ruin and back way whispered, Let go. Write, if you want to write.

3

I call a chapter of my life "the Rome years," not because it has any larger significance for others, but because the city has no rivals. Once I lived in Parma, I had no real reasons to return for extended stays, and thus the chapter closed. A special business train to Rome that stopped in our city meant that if I needed to attend a meeting or see an exhibit, I could board before seven in the morning and be back before ten at night. It took a family trip a few years ago to jolt me into a reverie of associations. Sitting with my husband and daughter in the gardens on the Aventine Hill, just beyond Santa Sabina and its fifth-century carved cedar doors, looking out across to Saint Peter's dome, I suddenly seemed to be touching those years as if I had never left. Out came memories of inclusion and out came that inner Tiber, a flow released then, of a curious, sensuous self, looking for definitions for women, for writers, for living a good life and a committed one. Out came the midwestern girl, as she called herself then. Out came the introspective thinker raised in an atmosphere of painful splits, who struggled to interpret the world, when her persona was that of a lighthearted rebel. This flood of memory began to appear as if it could be seen in present light, like the vast city below the hill, with its Roman forums and the view straight across all the roads and domes right to the high-. est point, Saint Peter's cupola. Of course there was traffic, too, and the periphery with its blighted concrete high-rises. The city, held together by a name, was barely an entity. It was multiplicity itself.

4

The Etruscan she-wolf that gazes out like a powerful icon in the papal rooms in the Capitoline Museum stands firmly with an open mouth, teeth pointed but not bared, just open, ready. Here is Rome's archaic, pagan birth mother. She is looking into the unknown, surveying for danger. And underneath her sharp teats are two bronze putti/children, added in the Renaissance. The Capitoline she-wolf, even if her authenticity is in dispute, holds the myth of Roman origins, having suckled Romulus and Remus after they were abandoned and left to die on the Palatine Hill. The mythical and realistic creature is one more element in the basic narrative of Rome about sustenance and survival. The salvation and nourish- ment offered by a wild animal and the salvation and nourishment offered by the Mother of God are paradigms of mothering and women that came up everywhere in Rome. Included in story after story, altar after altar, beauty and intense nurturing were ideals interpreted, expanded, and transgressed by lapse and excess.

As a young writer, I experienced the proliferation of ruins, statues, paintings, sultry nature as if the city were a maternal lap that cradled all human life, turning nothing and no one away. This indiscriminate abundance was a discovery, as it is for many northerners. People from northern cultures, who see themselves as independent searchers, no longer looking to a mother for indulgence and instruction, find themselves leaning into this fascinating and frustrating atmosphere. Rome's mixture of chaos and tolerance blurs distinctions, until finally, good and bad may coexist in the same definition. The she-wolf, the *lupa*, linked to darkness, in part, derives her name from the Greek word for light. Mary, the Mother of God, in her thousands of proliferations, is never depicted with a harsh expression in her eyes or on her lips.

5

In Rome's mild winters, on my way home after exciting walks next to the high walls flanking the river, I used to buy coal in a paper bag and burn the briquettes in a metal stove in my living room. The tiny wallpapered space with one modest window warmed up quickly, but when small gray mice dashed across the floor, nothing could make me feel comfortable. Once, before I found the nerve to set a neck-breaking trap, a large brown rat banged around in the closet for a week and made the room a source of dread.

I burned lumps of coal with prudence, counting them as if they were a substitute for meat, or fruit, since I had little money. In the late sixties, poverty was still an issue far more central to understanding Italian society than success. I embraced my new life as a way of exploring the meaning of society, tasting what being an intellectual meant, and how social justice could be part of the equation. Whatever my energies were, I assumed that once I learned more, they would lead me to my calling. I hungered to live in a place where artists had history and significance. I was a romantic, who had almost no female models. As writers before me who hovered over small sources of heat, I appreciated the scalding warmth of my little stove and the general condition of struggle. By the time the room was chilly again and I shoveled out papery ashes, it was clear that transformation, at least by fire, was a process with many stages.

The courtyard I lived in could not have been a more accurate expression of what was called then "the people." One passed through a stone and brick arch that took one away from the street, and life in the Middle Ages appeared on the other side of the entryway. Whether the enclosed circular space that worked like a theater in the round was always so noisy and contentious, I cannot say. I remember Signor Piero insisting it was quiet in the 1950s, until Rosina started talking at the window. I remember someone contradicting him and saying it was quiet as long as there were only Romans living in the space where mended sheets hung from the windows and bottles, cans, and sometimes objects as large as toilets crashed down onto the cobblestones. The chaos, according to him, started with the arrival of the Sicilians.

6

In the late sixties, the miniskirt that exposed women's legs in Oxford was not an acceptable style in Rome, especially if one was a
foreigner. I have long legs and didn't like the Romans' gawking
or, worse, the hands that they would try to slide along anything
above the knee, so it took only a few days before I dug through the
piles in an open market and found a dress with sleeves and a skirt
that fell to my calves.

Assumptions about a young woman living alone were often
voiced in the courtyard, where the low two-story houses with badly
peeling paint faced each other on three sides, bordered on the
fourth by a taller building of five floors. Indoor plumbing had been
added on to the latter in the fifties by sticking an external box-size
room, with a small window, to the exterior of each apartment. The
proximity of the apartments facing one another meant much of
the life going on inside was heard, if not seen. But much was seen,
too. Since all of the families had at least one member always
posted at a window, little of the life that went up and down my
staircase escaped them.

The external staircase leading to my front door was in full view. Like a prop in many operas, it was a place where every entry and exit was noted, and often mined for more significance than it had. In that sense, I had no privacy whatsoever. I was seen, judged, and all my moves were tracked by someone—Lucia, Signor Rolle, Minica. But there was no gossip. If an observation was made from one window to another, even in the night, when I might come in late or with a man, the remark, uncensored, was made loudly enough for all to hear.

"Do you like that man with a briefcase?"

"No, he's too thin."

"Do you think he's serious about the *americana*?"

"What do I know about her? And for that matter, what do I care?"

7

The external life on the stairs, the visible life of the young woman who was trying to define herself far from an Anglo-Saxon world, was one thing to me and another to the courtyard, where the stairs and all they revealed were a challenge. The courtyard observers, people who, to my mind, formed a kind of Greek chorus, followed my movements and, in spite of our differences, humanly let me in on their observations and concerns. At first, when I moved in, most people in the yard were worried or suspicious. As a foreign element, I was to be checked for any undesirable traits as well as followed because I might need help.

From the beginning, the people who began coming up my stairs provided startling contrast to the modest poverty of the residents. My visitors were students who appeared after I had an interview at an English-language teaching school, a few weeks after taking up residence in my apartment under the arch. Had the director hired me, I would have gotten the work permit I needed. "Oh no," the man had said, "you would be so bored teaching language. Let me send you private students. People do call us for tutors. I will just say you are part of the school. That way, you can keep all of the money for yourself."

His favor was unexplained. I did nothing special for the man and he asked nothing of me. His kindness forced me to continue working in *nero*, a widespread system that evades taxes but in my case meant I could not work legally. A steady stream of students trudged through the courtyard, which was usually ripe with the rotting remains of the fruit and vegetables that the vendors, who stored their carts for the Campo de' Fiori, dumped there and left for the furniture makers in the yard to sweep up. Rosina, my neighbor below, who lived in one room with damp walls and a lightbulb hanging from a cord on the ceiling, would usually announce them with a shout.

"Io," was how the courtyard people coped with my name. "Io,"

she would cry out with her Roman accent, which made my name sound like *eeeee ooooo*, "the man with the black beard" or "the girl with thick legs is coming up to see you." Then she would return to her nearly constant purpose, droning the Rosary. "Hail Mary, full of grace, the Lord is with thee. Blessed art thou among women, and blessed is the fruit of thy womb, Jesus." She spindled and spun the prayer all day long, until someone screamed for her to stop.

8

The majority of people who appeared at my door belonged to the class of Roman nobility called "Black" because of Church connections and perhaps, more recently, possibly Fascist ones. Most, undoubtedly, had never frequented such a humble corner of Rome. They found it colorful that an American would settle in such a place. One of my intense and demanding students, not one of the nobility, was a man who always asked for more assignments. He became the head of the Bank of Italy and now is one of the most powerful men in Europe, the leader of the European Central Bank. Most who came were Roman princes and princesses, who assumed that I was an employee of the prestigious language institution they had contacted. After some months of lessons, many arrived with gifts of clothing or food because they worried I was not taking care of myself. Their kindness was real and comforting. It was flattering, too. Some sent packages anonymously (although they were easily deciphered), having delivery people bring an extravagant coat or dress in a showy box from a store with a fancy name, or spectacular baskets of fruit wrapped in cellophane. The gifts arrived without the sender's name attached, so as not to offend my pride. My courtyard neighbors would explode with curiosity and operatic speculations about weddings and what I could possibly do with the bold satin ribbons or a mountain of cadaver-colored fruits that were then foreign to my neighbors, who shopped exclusively in the open market. Furry and exotic, kiwis always created a stir. "What are those gray balls?" "Did you see?"

None of my noble students commented on the yard or the darkness of the small room where we sat at the round table and corrected exercises. Either they were good sports or their education included the ability to give the impression that they were at ease. Their formal manners were, by and large, defined by the enormous Renaissance palaces in which they lived, waited upon by servants. Our conversations were often mundane and slightly boring ones about taking private planes to ski resorts or eating midnight meals at clubs, which made getting up anytime before noon problematic. One young noble aspired to attend an American university, and when he and I filled out his applications, he asked me if he should list Gianni Agnelli or Queen Elizabeth as references, or if an American like Henry Ford II would be more useful. When I said they might prefer an academic's letter or one from his supervisor at work, he rebuffed the suggestion, complaining that I must not understand the system.

My midwestern way of reading life made the students exotic subjects about whom I was curious, and I did long for friends. In the end, though, after saying yes a few times to evenings at their country clubs and flights on their private planes, I knew theirs was not a style of life that interested me. My refusal to let them pay my way had an element of pride in it, but the realization that I needed focuses expressing my own concerns was the stronger reason for my being deterred. I was happy feeding a growing but not indiscriminate hunger to learn. My American relatives, who hoped for a Broadway climax out of *The King and I*, couldn't understand that I was trying to get away from unreal solutions that plagued much thinking about women's lives—including, of course, that of finding a rich Roman noble for a husband.

The way Minica, Lucia, and Signor Rolle unrolled time in the courtyard with little concern for its contents or direction—"Is it ten o'clock?" "How do I know?" "Have you heard the bell?" "No, have you?" "Do you think it broke?" "How could all the bells break at once?" "Have you heard the bell, then, even one?"—was idleness that contrasted with my sense of how time might be spent. Yet the extravagant dimensions of my nobility's boredom—people who could have had anything—were sadder to me, even if their solutions for spending time were no surprise. The princes and princesses continued to come and we would laugh together, often over unfinished assignments. They paid and wanted to pay, even when they never appeared for lessons. When they stopped in spontaneously, usually quite late at night, I would wave and wish them good times as their fast little sports cars (one, an Alfa Spider garnered at the gambling tables of Monte Carlo) sped off to the countryside, with its promises of Thoroughbreds, swimming pools, drugs, and starry nights. Not by chance, sober volumes of Gramsci and Pasolini were my bedtime reading.

9

The steps leading to my front door often radiated the pungent odor of cats. The lack of money or culture to sterilize any of them meant many were doomed from birth. The courtyard cats, if they were not calling in heat, were often crying out in pain, dying slow, terrible deaths from poisoning. Rosina fed the milling hordes under her window white spongy chopped calf's lung and prayed for them, chastising the furniture makers, who were assumed to deliver the poison. I, too, left scraps and would often find five or six sleeping in front of the door. They were a sadly fluctuating population, noisy, aggressive, wild, often patchy from fleas or mange. They belonged to no one, and the kittens came forth three times a year and mostly died of starvation. I did favor a little black one, whom I named Gamba. I let her enter the house, and many times other cats would climb over my roof and enter a second-story window and push Gamba out. Often Minica would have seen the crime. "The gray bad one, Testaccio, balanced on the window and boxed her till she fell." Having been neutered, she found it more difficult to defend herself.

The steps, marked as they were by feline life, needed attention every day, so that my students could make the climb without being knocked out by the scent of spore. A bucket of soapy water, thrown from the door, was my solution. Not precisely the Tivoli Gardens, but the water dropping from step to step was a spectacle I liked. Once as I hurled it down, a man who had been sent to me by the school, a man who had won a Nobel Prize, was on the stairs; Rosina had not yet announced him. His blue suit and shiny shoes were violently soaked. I was speechless until Marcello, a rather vicious workman who glued furniture together, began to laugh. A man in the outdoor toilet on the third floor lifted his hat. My hatted neighbor, a butcher who slaughtered sheep in Yugoslavia and then drove the truckload of dead animals back into Italy to sell, had spied the scene and what in his mind could only be sparks of romance. "*Accidenti, che rabbia*" (roughly translated: "Jeeeez, what fury!"), he observed, full of awed admiration. The distinguished scientist came in just long enough to wipe off his suit.

10

Another Roman nobleman, with a leonine baritone, in his seventies when he came to me, fully embraced the atmosphere of the courtyard, even snatching a mouse with his hand as it skittered over his shoes while we worked at the table. Wearing white suits that reflected his white hair and set off his strong, large features, he loved the scene, although he lived in one of the most beautiful squares in Rome. The famous fountain with the four Bernini turtles balanced on the fingers of youths dripped day and night in front of his palace door. In centuries gone by, it often had been the only source of water for the Jews in the surrounding ghetto.

The noble was an agronomist, and we translated a book into English that he had written for use in Cuba. "Come with me," he said quite often. "I'll introduce you to Fidel and let you see how my irrigation system works on depleted soil." "Come," he would say,

"Cuba is beautiful and Fidel is a smart man." Of course I was deeply curious to see Cuba and meet Fidel Castro, but my U.S. passport forbade me from going. Besides that, I was not even legal in Italy. Yet that sense of being able to get close to a new source, a new world, traveling with someone who actually worked there, remained tempting. Marxism was a system that many intellectuals seriously tried to analyze for its alternative applications in the developing world. It was a language many found cogent. Italy had the largest Communist Party in Europe. I was involved, like part of my generation, in resisting the U.S. presence in Vietnam, attending rallies in Rome's Fascist-built suburb, EUR, where thousands of workers and students waved banners for Ho Chi Minh. But Cuba was not a cause I could take on. "I can't," I would say; "unfortunately, I can't." "You are just like Kennedy," he would retort. "Like Jack and then Bobby. *Imperialista, capitalista*," he would admonish, his mouth opening into a huge joking smile, his beautiful teeth as white as the oxen used in the south to plow. "You are afraid of Communists."

Against his skin, umber from supervising work in scorching fields, his smile made his face even more striking. His language sent off sparks and flamed with meanings, putting intriguing distance between us. Words carried, sometimes as illusion, sometimes as fact, whole identities.

11

It was soon after a murder in a hotel on the same street onto which the courtyard opened, and several violent demonstrations against the war in Vietnam, during which tear gas marked the walls even inside my little house, that word passed that the police were cracking down on foreigners. The genuine discomfort of being illegal arose again, and the solution seemed to be to apply for a work permit. But to go to the police, in the central *questura* building, was daunting, since I had been outside the law for over a year.

I had been told I could not say I was giving private lessons. "No one will believe you. They will think you are a prostitute. No one will believe a young woman can live by giving private lessons." I decided to say, since there were no demands for receipts (comprehensive income tax laws did not yet exist), that I lived on earnings from writing. The idea thrilled me. By that time, I had written some short stories about a young woman who loses her father in America, and one about Russian and American astronauts who have shared visions of death in outer space. These certainly reflected some of my experience: the death of my father, when I was nineteen, and a continuing interest in anti–Cold War politics. And outer space, looking at things from far-off perspectives that made earthly life seem resolved, was a habit of survival that I had had from childhood. But much had changed in that first year.

I had arrived in Rome, with five ten-pound notes, having abruptly decided to give up a tenured teaching post at the technical college in Oxford. I left on the spur of the moment to escape a marriage I could no longer accept. I stayed for a few days in what has historically been called "a fleabag hotel." Possibly because the mattresses were still made of straw, really nasty creatures inhabited that category of accommodation. I had no other choice if I wanted to avoid asking my family for money. There were problems at home, but it was pride and habit that shaped my decision to refrain. My mother had cut all support, including that for my college education, when my father died very suddenly of a heart attack. In a family that insisted that women should never work, almost as if it were a moral dogma, I became self-supporting overnight.

On my own in Rome, I found that I had to lie. It was an awkward turn; I knew a lot about omissions, but inventing truth was new. Yet the writer in me had interpreted much of family and political life as stories and, in that sense, I did not have to reach too far to come up with some convenient narratives. In the following weeks, I never said that I was married and needed work, because I had the clothes on my back and a diminishing small supply of cash. At twenty-six, facing the terrible pain of a failed relation-ship, I needed independence in order to reestablish a sense of who I was.

My first request, the day after I arrived, my red, swollen eyes hidden behind sunglasses, was at the UN branch for Food and Agriculture, along the blue Laurentina Metro line. That foray took place a month before moving into the courtyard and a good six weeks before visiting the language school. I asked if the food agency had work for writers. Kindness, again, flares in my memory. An Australian said he could hire me for technical writing but that he would need proof of my trade. I bluffed. "My trunks have not yet arrived," I said, as if I were a nineteenth-century lady taking the grand tour. "That's where my writing is. I've published many things—poems, essays, lots of articles." If the Internet had existed my tale would have been checked there and then. Instead, I pushed forward. "I am working on a short story, so perhaps if I could show you that . . ."

12

The hotel clerk, who tapped out receipts on a little spidery black box with terraces of black keys covered in plastic and an elegant but worn red-and-black-striped ribbon, agreed to let me use his table in off-hours, once he had completed his work. He usually put his head down on the front counter around nine-thirty, and from then on, I could sit at his table and copy my handwritten pages onto my little portable typewriter, and revise them if necessary. He let me return to work in that quiet space even after I moved on to a cheaper room in a boardinghouse three days after I arrived.

My determination and guilelessness about why I was in Rome, as well as the unexplainable, sympathetic moves of others at cru-cial moments, helped me finish my short story and hand it to the officer at the agency, as if I lived off royalties and could pay for caissons of trunks. The freelance contract for writing two filmstrips on planting techniques and a paper on the controversial green revolution was enough, in dollars, to sustain me for more than eight months. It let me put down a deposit for the apartment in the courtyard and leave the communal room in a Roman flat. The rented room, too, had had a mattress with bugs; I received a fair number of stings from small biting spiders. The bathroom and its bar of soap were shared by ten. The TV in the dark living space blasted day and night. The main room drew its light from the flicker of the screen. No wonder that I felt buoyed and optimistic as I left the rather Soviet communal arrangement.

13

The moment of truth before the clerk who was to listen to my request for a work permit seemed fraught with a more consequential kind of feigned confidence than the tale a year earlier had been that had gotten me the FAO contract. After all, the document I was pursuing was issued by the municipal police. As I calmly said, "I am a writer. That is my work," my chest tightened. The half lie I told him felt like an animal sticking its nose out of a cave that was finally being abandoned. My heart pounded as I declared my profession to the government. I also felt intrigued (that way I had of looking at myself as another person), wondering if, by confessing this wish to a clerk, I might be brutally expelled from the city.

Looking at these moments from a distance that has reversed so many of my perspectives and concerns, I feel a gentle affection. The strictness and judgment, fear and sadness of a large element in my Protestant childhood education went up in smoke that afternoon. The meaning of honesty was redefined by the exhilarating shock and power of uncensored sincerity: the outsized enthusiasm of the clerk's imagination; his confidence that women should be writers; my own public declaration. Unhindered by literal facts (which up until that point had been for me the clearest divide between truth and lies), I entered a new world. The clerk handed me a pen to dip in a crusty bottle of ink. "Here," he said, eyes glowing with admiration, "write what I tell you." Raised in a conservative Republican family with strict Lutheran underpinnings, and having a U.S. senator for a grandfather, I was always in full possession of clear guidelines for public accountability. I became a participant, if that is the right word, an accomplice, if that is more accurate, in an action that might be considered a crime.

He began to dictate. What followed is one untranslatable way that Italy challenges with flexibility and fantasy those who live on its soil. It goes deeper than words and could be seen as combustible fuel. It goes a long way toward illuminating how Italian hearts and minds work, on both dark and light paths. It cannot necessarily be defended. But it needs to be described.

A river of speech poured into the dull room. It was ornate, rich with memories, dreams, proud connections to the city. The clerk, obviously with aspirations of his own, waited as I formed his phrases in Italian. He nodded approvingly when I got the spelling right and would correct words when I missed a double letter, those sounds that still elude me.

> I came to Rome because I was a writer and I needed the inspiration of ancestors, the classical world, the sound of feet on stones, the color of the marine pines and the cypress, so darkly expressive of death. I came to Rome for its pomegranates and its ruins, so often frescoes with symbols and gardens and garlands and love. . . . I came for its lovers, and tragic endings, its heroines with courage and wit. Rome was the only place I could write, because it was the only place where real artists could create, and therefore I needed permission to stay long enough to bring my novels to light.

We had rushed along for nearly four pages before we reached my aspiration to write novels in the plural. I loved the Ovid part. I had not heard of Vittoria Colonna, but I was glad to hear she was a friend to Michelangelo. I cherished his words on heroines and tragic endings. Cicero, whom he called "a giant," I had read on my own, and Horace, as well. I had seen Rossellini's film *Rome, Open City*, which he announced as my model for realism in modern times. But when he ventured into the rapturous claim that I would write several novels, my midwestern training about the strict relation between words and reality brought me up short: What I was doing was against the law. What if a policeman climbed my stairs one day to check? Couldn't I say that I hoped to write a single book?

"No," he said, with a sweep of dismissal. "You need time. You can't say just one book. What is one book? They won't believe you. You must stay until you cannot lose what you find in Rome. You must live and be a writer until it burns and you express that fire."

He asked me to recopy the text so that on the lined paper, made official by affixing tax stamps, my Italian would look fluent and correct. "Now, read it out loud," he soberly commanded. Each sentence caused me anguish and giddy pleasure.

My declaration to join with beauty, to become part of a community that extended far beyond me, made him smile with satis-

faction. "*Bello. Bellissimo*," he interjected, and then he listened intently before giving one final hushed judgment. I finished reading the text that had brought the two of us together, binding us and releasing our pompous but reverent paean into the collective sea of artistic aspiration. "*Bene*," he said, crossing his arms over his chest. "No, not *bene*. Marvelous!"

The clerk quickened his step and disappeared into the depths of the next room. As he left, I half-assumed that no one would ever accept such rhetoric. When he returned, he was waving a four-year permit to work. I think of what the lines of immigrants would do for that permit now and burn with shame. Or rather, I remind myself that Italy hasn't changed that much. In present-day Italy, I, along with many professional friends, try to compensate the need to be legal by signing papers in order to help domestic immigrant workers obtain their status. There is a breathtaking gap, a metaphysical canyon, between what is considered moral and what is considered legal in Italy, not only in institutional cases, when abuse is rampant, but in everyday practice, when compassion or charity is part of the solution. When filling out forms, the clerk will often be the one to suggest the way to get around a rule.

In its way, my *permesso* request was about survival, too. The sixties were years in which independence of mind was hard-fought ground for women. By putting my profession into words and signing a pact in Rome, I crossed a line. I had sworn that I was in my two-room house to become a writer. The massive oath put into my mouth by a Roman who understood art as its own higher law, reaching back as far as prehistoric sunrises and sunsets and putting forward his favorites among the classics, now stands winnowed and clean, lightened of all its encumbering weight: what it meant when I felt frightened by what I had signed. Now it shines with another interpretation. It holds the beginning of my understanding of commitment. At the time, I was rightly worried about the pages, their falsity and the obviousness of that. I knew that truth often resided in bold ventures defined by purity of intent and willingness to carry through, but I had not yet recognized that my own life would often claim those latter grounds. Even if the actual permit (there were no Xeroxes) has been lost in one of my moves, it still signals the beginning of my acceptance of the tensions in truth. This was not an anecdote, although it had folkloric aspects. It was a binding act bringing me face-to-face with new powers, risks, and levels of decision.

I cannot remember a single feature of the clerk's face. Memory does not always retain what we would prefer. But how could I ever forget such passion? The clerk, in that dull place, where the obvious writers to cite would have been Svevo or Kafka, gave me a push that has lasted a lifetime. By leading with his heart and imagination, he guided me toward a crucial angle in truth. He made me braver and lighter as I started to connect with how a writer lives.

14

I began this book with a truck driver's frustration and my own. Those interminable five minutes of incomprehension were probably my first consciousness of a different culture and what it means not to understand what's in a word. To set university learning aside and feel the shallow feebleness of my expectations for reality, especially when confronted with an enormous physical feature, a river running through the city and through time, had an effect that still works as a check on me when I enter a different culture. *Tevere.* I came to respect it as a life-giving artery in the history of Rome. And I learned the importance of knowing where I really was by standing on its banks.

As a young girl in Wisconsin, I had waded in creeks and fished for crabs, emerged with teeth chattering and skin shriveled blue from staying too long in glacial lakes, but the possibility of merging with a river's living power had never happened before Rome. I visited the Tiber almost daily, as if it were a shrine. Its moods of drift and rush were only two among hundreds. This reading of life, using my mind's eye, is an experience that still alerts me to change and flow as constants. It lies deep, uncluttered by words. The Tiber, though held by its banks and borders, told an unshapable story every day. I absorbed the wide perspective of what it means to live the experience of an ancient river. Two observations that have stayed with me: It's never empty and never pitch-black.

III

Tombs and Chapels

"You take delight not in a city's seven or seventy wonders, but in the answer it gives to a question of yours."
"Or the question it asks you, forcing you to answer, like Thebes through the mouth of the Sphinx."

—Marco Polo and Kublai Khan speaking in Italo Calvino,
Invisible Cities (translated by William Weaver)

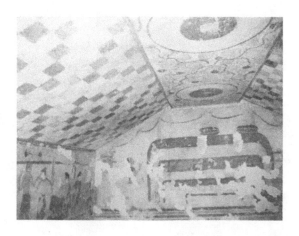

1

In Rome, Michelangelo's work occasions its own pilgrimage. When I arrived in the city, his *Pietà* in Saint Peter's Basilica had not yet been attacked by a madman who thought he was Christ, smashing the Madonna's arm at the elbow and chipping her nose and right eyelid. The young and beautiful Maria was not under bullet-proof glass as hordes swarmed around her. When I came to Rome, Michelangelo's name—and all it promised—was not the only synonym for the city, though certainly his work represented the apex of what defined Italian genius.

His immaculate *Pietà* in Saint Peter's; the mobbed Sistine Chapel bejeweled with his staggering intuitions, the revealing Old Testament images, the sibyls and the tensions of dire prophecy;

the massive statue of Moses in St. Peter in Chains that reflects Michelangelo's harsh and unshakable sense of the law and of human failure; Saint Peter's Basilica capped by the overwhelming masculine dome he had redesigned; the surprising, unremarkable Christ carrying the cross in Santa Maria Sopra Minerva; the official sublimity of his public social spaces: the Campidoglio, the Capitoline piazza rising above the Roman forums and facing away, toward St. Peter's—a generous open invitation to view the city; the monumental staircase leading up to that piazza; the third floor of the Farnese palace, near my old home, where he had also planned a bridge to cross the Tiber from the palace; his copious unfinished projects, meticulous detailed plans that sometimes were turned into reality, like the renovation of Porta Pia, a gate in the Aurelian Walls—all contain such energy that they stand out like rockets lifting off their launching pads. The enormous blasts of originality and purpose palpably shake those who stand to gaze and think.

Yet even Michelangelo is unable to dominate the past and present rumble of politics in Rome. He is forced over and over into creating the elegantly massive, the significantly grand: his herculean efforts pushed and pressed by taskmaster rulers hungry and impatient for his talent to mirror their power. I can't recognize the human artist in most of his work in Rome, the human being, often broken, usually torn and dissatisfied. I can't equate his supreme Roman works with the man who challenges stone, shapes its unyielding, brittle nature into fluid shapes that emit human sounds. In Rome, few of his marble subjects seep with groans, the involuntary weeping, pain, antagonisms that his fingers could command.

The unfinished *Prisoners*, which are in Florence and Paris today, were originally destined for Giulio II's tomb in Rome. Those settled in the Boboli Gardens and later, in the early 1900s, installed in the Accademia lend to Florence compelling images of Michelangelo's traits. Perhaps if they had reached their original destination in Rome, they would have changed my overall obser-

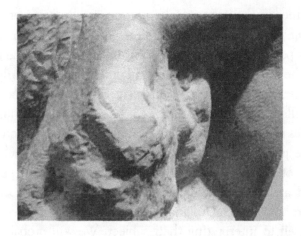

vations about where to find his essence. The sculptor's unmade decisions in the six blocks of stone lining the corridor leading to the *David* query that statue and release questions, which, like birds startled by noise, fly and bump against the walls. Taken together, the two contrasting periods of work and their final results provide not only a wrenching picture of the process of sculpting but a powerful portrait of the man.

The fact is that in Rome, Michelangelo was dragged away from his first love, sculpting. The Sistine Chapel and the sacrifices it entailed, sacrifices that were wrung from him by Giulio II, stupefy viewers nearly five centuries later. His growing ability to solve technical and compositional problems in the Sistine Chapel can be traced as Michelangelo moves across the ceiling from his first scene, *The Flood*. The inventiveness of his compositions and their expressions are revelations. But the distance of the ceiling from its viewers, which defines the difficulty of its creation and the synthetic nature of the emotions of the story, is almost symbolic of how much he had to give up in order to solve the problems he had been asked to address. The feeling between Adam and God, whose index fingers reach toward each other, an image that is as famous as the Mona Lisa's smile or the hourglass shape of a Coke bottle, is reexamined in the image of Christ's arms in the fresco of the *Last Judgment*. One arm is lifted in righteous condemnation, and the other is positioned protectively in front of his body. The gap between the first touch of God and Adam grows until, nearly thirty years later, Christ on the far wall of the Sistine Chapel becomes a beast. Filled with despairing anger as he sits, looking at humanity, he judges most with wrath. The relational hand is no more.

The physical and psychological processes in Michelangelo's activity of working stone and his tendency to leave parts unfinished are well documented, even in the artist's papers. The *Prisoners* hold a special fascination because of their rawness, which lends itself to interpreting their subject. We will probably never know the artist's intentions; the figures are unfinished. But their halfway state perfectly suggests the physical effort and confinement of men who were forced to labor as prisoners or slaves. The viewer cannot help but realize that Michelangelo bore similar burdens in Rome. The unhewn stone that presses on the prisoner's head, which he is forced to lift although he cannot stand, the statue of San Matteo, whose chest nearly bursts from the effort of resistance—these contorted poses express the torment and blind suffering inherent in extreme motion and forced work. As

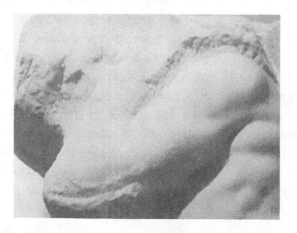

the prisoners twist, coerced by their destiny, they wait to emerge from brutal hammer strokes and surfaces that are unyielding.

In Rome, too often, Michelangelo is sacrificed to resolve social, practical, and sometimes rhetorical problems. He finds spectacular and massive solutions. The messages, especially in his architecture, are about grandeur, sublimity, and official drama, using languages revived from the classical world. His patrons ask little from him in terms of his more personal interpretations of hope and human suffering. Perhaps because he is captured by three Popes, Giulio II, Clemente VII, and Paolo III, who absorb him in Church projects that often limit his time for sculpting, or perhaps because the Church sponsors so many geniuses, Michelangelo amazes and offers unforgettable solutions, nearly unimaginable in scope. But he cannot do more than contribute greatly to the public experience of Rome's variegated layers and to its capacity to suggest the eternal. In Rome, even Michelangelo pours into a crowded flow of restored history that is always finding the next

Mithraic altar or unveiling the Baroque billows of another restored façade. I felt the encroaching competition confining him when I first saw the then uncleaned, tallow-colored Sistine Chapel. Along the lower walls are works by Pietro Perugino, Sandro Botticelli, Domenico Ghirlandaio, Cosimo Rosselli, Luca Signorelli. Raffaello Sanzio was attracting the Pope's attention and painting for him as Michelangelo reluctantly raised the ingenious self-designed scaffolding for holding himself and his assistants up.

2

In Florence, instead, this man emerges as an essence of the city— its intelligence and creativity; its masculine, or, as Mary McCarthy calls it, its "bachelor" point of view. In Florence, he dominates it as the sculptor he was born to be. In Florence, although he designs several major monuments, it is the marble he works into human forms that defines his influence. In Florence, Michelangelo shapes visions of human reality: in the *David*, which expresses the physical and psychological dimension of youth's power; in the inverted perspective of celestial cycles in the Medici tombs, where *Day* and *Night*, *Dawn* and *Dusk* define the dimensions between eternity and human life. The figures of Lorenzo and Giuliano de' Medici are placed above their tombs only to observe motions that dwarf their reigns. The number of sculptures Michelangelo creates in Florence is nearly twice that done in Rome. His works, including some in wood, like the early crucifix now in Santo Spirito, often evoke, through beautifully accurate human forms, compassion and sympathy. He finds and embraces the tension between sublimity and reality's effects on human beings. He masters the contradictory task of replicating being alive by finding metaphor in his material. His polychrome crucifix, the Bandini *Pietà* with its nearly finished Christ in the Duomo museum, and the clay and wood model of the *River God* in the Casa Buonarroti are made from different materials but emerge from hands born to physically shape three dimensions.

In Florence, marble, however, is the material through which Michelangelo monstrously releases awe. Working that material into luminous bodies, even when he stops short of finishing, he finds positions and subjects to express freedom and potential. His work thunders with the process of release. It throws off the wondrous fallout of human energy mirroring creation itself. In Florence, Michelangelo, the man and his work, fuse, so that a viewer's brain feels as if a cosmic cluster has been brought up close enough to inspect it. Michelangelo finds places to stop in works and these stops take viewers even further into his imagination. David has not yet hurled the stone. We must imagine Goliath as a Titan because of the size of David and the intense concentration and worry on his brow. Michelangelo's vision of art originates in a mind that, even when work has been completed, suggests unseen power that is larger still.

Mary McCarthy wrote, "Florence is a city of endurance, a city of stone." The terse description passes on the succinctness of Florence and sets its male or "monkish" severity in sharp contrast to Rome's bounteous, colored flow. Yet Michelangelo expresses his more feminine side in the works remaining in Florence. Rereading McCarthy, I wondered if she wasn't hemmed in by proving her own cultural point, a moment in time when she saw women as gaining space, when she wrote about Florence as "bachelor." Nevertheless, Rome, with its curves and domes, its solace in color and light, its emptying and filling spaces that most often are rounded, could never be called stark or monkish. All along the boulevards shaded by plane trees with their green-and-yellow giraffelike bark and their gaudy leaves drifting down to the dawdling river, it's hard not to see Rome's voluptuous beauty and the kind and cruel ways it ages as traits traditionally attributed to women.

3

Visiting Rome now, I rarely get much further than the ancient Romans. This attraction was real from the moment I decided to stay. Still more riveting then was the beauty and vitality of even earlier times, times not obscured completely by the Romans. In the early years, at least for short periods, I was content just reveling in what remained of the Etruscans. The beauty and apparent sincerity of Etruscan art, its portrayal of sacredness as energy possessed by all living things, held warm and appealing revelations in comparison with the powerful, rational definitions and techniques of the Greeks and Romans that were the basis of the Renaissance. The balance between life and death that animated Etruscan images was not about rational learning.

The smiling life-size terra-cotta couple that occupies a central place in the Etruscan Museum, inside of the Villa Guilia, Pope Giulio III's palace, was a favorite spot of mine to encounter this view. The woman, wearing pointed reddish clay slippers, and the man, framed by an amusing pointed beard and bare feet, rest against each other as they look out into a dimension of life that assumes there is something to see in the invisible. Their bright gaze im-

prints a feeling for this world and the next. "Tell me," I always wanted to whisper, and then, following their eyes' apparent focus, I realized that their expression answers that question. Their complicity as they gaze at death precedes all operas and heroic arias about lovers and their tragic separations. No sandpit or trapdoor here. No last judgment or flames. In their illuminated faces, Yeats's glittering eyes dance with serenity and connectedness. Eternity is music that plays. Full of anticipation, their reclining bodies, tilted in part to a sitting position, suggest a life of physical closeness, of lovemaking that bound them in satisfaction. Women in Etruscan times operated in society on terms of equality unknown anywhere else for centuries. This luminous couple knew each other well on Earth.

4

The first Etruscan tombs I visited were in Cerveteri, just outside of Ostia Antica. I went with a British couple during the first months I lived in Rome. There, among large earth-covered tumuli, burial ruins composed a miniature stone city with little streets. I ducked my head into what could be thought of as small houses with pointed tufa roofs and inside them saw narrow tufa beds with tufa pillows. D. H. Lawrence's fascination with the Etruscans followed me as we wandered in that city of the dead, with its nearly ten thousand tombs. "Oh build your ship of death. Oh build it! / for you will need it. / For the voyage of oblivion awaits you." The appealing domestic structures built from the ubiquitous volcanic rock had long since lost their frescoed visions and the little dishes and accoutrements to be carried and used in the next world. Doors propped and cracked open and walls cleansed by sunlight remained. Some with imitation carved beams and latticed ceilings were visible. They were sweet little homes. The red-skinned divers and dancing leopards found in other Etruscan cities were gone, even as strokes of color. Occasionally one of the tombs with frescoes was opened for viewing, the most famous being that of the Rilievi family, third century B.C.E. But that day, the plain chambered tombs were sufficient to suggest a culture that offered soothing and even happy solutions, as Lawrence wrote, "fitting and ready for the departed soul." From the Etruscans' evolving style of burial came the Roman way of building tombs above- and belowground. (They also borrowed from the Greeks.) But the Romans extinguished the Etruscan feeling for mystery, exchanging it for images of power.

Located at the mouth of the Tiber, the port of Ostia, used before Roman times, became a thriving commercial center for the Romans. Ostia Antica was the destination for the granite columns essential for the construction of the Pantheon. Quarried in Egypt, floated to Alexandria, transferred to vessels that sailed to Ostia, sixteen forty-foot-high, sixty-ton columns were rolled onto barges there and floated on the Tiber to Rome. At its height the Roman city was a thriving center of over sixty thousand people. Then it was slowly abandoned; the position on the sea, beginning in the fourth century C.E., gradually silted in. The amount of Etruscan influence that survived and in what ways and proportions is

still a source of much uncertainty and speculation. How Etruscan time and customs were absorbed into the Roman period, when the Etruscans were conquered and their culture suppressed, is not easy to imagine in the Roman port, except as near-total extermination. The beautiful ruins at Ostia are identifiably Roman in layout, and the construction of red brick is theirs, lacking only traditional marble façades stripped by Renaissance builders in Rome. The town model is well known, and communicates efficiency. The open tombs of the Etruscan city of Cerveteri, of course, tell a story central to all of human existence, but that elevated cemetery is all that stands of a vast settlement.

Cerveteri emerged in my mind as nearly magical when compared with the beautifully preserved Roman Ostia. The British couple had brought a picnic in a straw basket, since we planned to visit both places in one day. We ate our bread and cheese and drank our red wine in the Etruscan burial grounds, without feeling any gloom. There was green grass and birdsong. There was a simple welcome emanating from the benign domestic structures. In these two incredibly well-preserved places, close in time and distance, so little remained of the Etruscans' wider civilization. The evidence had been taken away, erased, their visions defied, and yet in the Etruscan city of the dead, as we sat on low stone walls, they felt close, alive, soft, as if they had never left.

IV

Layers

But the unfading, abiding whites, blues, greens, and gold of the winemakers remain transparent messengers of the Roman spirit of health
and pleasure.

1

In Rome, even when churches are bolted tight for long lunches, there is much that amuses on exciting façades and in charming angles. But when the churches reopen, after those dead hours, there is no end to what speaks, setting the mind afire, engaging it with questions of history and aesthetics.

The gap before my evening lessons held possibilities for searches—"pit stops," I might have called them then, where the fuel to be added was culture. One favorite included catacombs. Mounting a bus near the Campo de' Fiori in the early afternoon, I often traveled along the Via Nomentana, rich in palm trees and unbelievably large embassies, a ride of nearly an hour in traffic, just to spend another hour in green gardens and among playing children while waiting to enter simple buildings that held within one set of walls the transition between the Roman Empire and Christianity's first centuries.

Inside the high walls were two edifices spanning close to eighteen hundred years. There was the mid-fourth-century mausoleum of Santa Costanza, built by the first Christian emperor for his daughter Costanza and possibly for a second daughter. The mausoleum expressed in its architecture and decoration the symbols of early, official Christianity. Outside and down the path on the right was a church built to cover the second-century catacombs, including the remains of Sant'Agnese.

2

Erected in the seventh century, over the ruins of the earlier church, Sant'Agnese opens around four, when the usually hard-to-find guide returns to take visitors into the catacombs that were outlawed and closed in the fifth century and then became the reason for the seventh-century construction. The guide exists, above all, to prevent little flocks of observers from getting lost in the maze of more than six kilometers of tunnels. She walks them through a few short passages and winds them safely through the blind angles of the hollowed-out tufa ceiling-to-floor shelves that feel like library stacks.

I descended only three or four times in all my early visits to Sant'Agnese. The catacombs, besides being musty, were heavy on the heart. Instead, in the rounded aboveground mausoleum of Santa Constanza, the magical, somewhat naïve pictures of peacocks and festoons and elfish winemakers crushing grapes in the ambulatory ring outside the columns supporting the dome offer unlimited delight and pleasure. At the time they were made, their rustic images still fit a formula for depicting everyday life in Rome. They came to be seen as pertaining to a different culture as Christianity grew in successive centuries. Inside that same mausoleum

in the two apses, the pictures of Christ as Pantocrator, a temporal and heavenly ruler, one with an inscription "The Lord Contains the Law," are radical announcements of the intricate overlaps created as temporal power was reorganized. They remain a significant example of art as well as political and religious history.

The mosaics, textured patterns of small colored stones, cut and fitted for the centuries, never ceased to attract me and others who might be called "pilgrims," young and old people with fingers in guidebooks, who appeared on their own, without a tour group. The mosaics in the whole complex, including one of Sant'Agnese in the church bearing her name, largely predate the marvels in Ravenna, and display accomplishment as well as arresting religious visions. But the unfading, abiding whites, blues, greens, and gold of the winemakers remain transparent messengers of the Roman spirit of health and pleasure. Forward-looking, athletically pagan, connected to agriculture and cyclical nature, they enchant with their immediate rendering of joy and celebration, as well as commemorating a few virtuous citizens and donors. In that subtle use of tiny pieces of colored glass and stone, the artisans imagined permanence, and yet, how could they have imagined us, so far away in time, still delighted by them?

3

The seventh-century church, farther down the path, holds bones that were identified as belonging to Sant'Agnese, a beloved martyr in Rome, beheaded at the age of twelve in the second century for refusing to marry a Roman official who would not convert. She was buried outside the walls of Rome in the first catacombs, which eventually expanded to house more than thirty thousand corpses. Christians who followed Sant'Agnese's example, first as martyrs and later as officially established Christian families who, nevertheless, wanted to be buried in the way of martyrs, made it necessary to continuously extend the underground crypts. These living seams reveal pictures of time and of institutions searching for practices, disclosing meanings and symbols both physical and metaphysical. The fusion between two political and social orders from the late Roman Empire to a developing early Church can be navigated in this green and quiet complex and be seen as an essential summary. To rest on a bench in the garden was to take in a transition from one world to another made real by its physical overlaps and borrowings. It still invites one to imagine lives then and now, when social revolution involves religious identity.

4

The church of Sant'Agnese has been reworked, as have the catacombs below it. Originally hollowed out of red tufa, which was then sold to make blocks that are seen in all Roman construction, the vertical stacks of slots are difficult to explain in terms of the emotion they stir up. Empty, dark, and repetitive shelves going on and on, they can seem, at moments, to echo, as images, the stacks of beds in the overcrowded prison camps of World War II.

The guide usually took visitors into one room that stood for the whole. During one descent, I saw a room belonging to a family whose graves occupied all three walls. Here and there a human touch: a carved symbol, a dove, some form of Latin inscription explaining the death of a two-year-old daughter. I found solace in the scratched crosses and small stone altar. The tales of lions and little Agnese's unwavering last prayers were not really comprehensible to me when I was young. While today I am quite awed by the nuances of sacrifice and its ramifications in nonviolent protest, I remain unable to see any glorification in violence endured.

5

When I visited the catacombs in the Rome years, I found myself willfully trying to fit them into what I knew about persecution and human liberty. Excitement about the Catholic Church and its doctrines was alive. Vatican II and its articulation of ecumenical dialogue was intellectual fare that often overlapped with Marxist thinking. But my excursions were about curiosity, stops to see what early Christianity felt like, more than visits propelled by faith. My head was bowed because the ceilings of the primitive belowground chambers were low. Reddish black walls and cramped spaces bore witness to a time in history when Christianity was a practice that was dangerous and still defining itself. The premises of those labyrinths were stark and unrhetorical. They spoke of a religion that often required life-altering choices, fanatical sacrifices, and courage.

The philosophy based on love of God and one's neighbor seemed more dangerous than hopeful in the catacombs. Yet its mystery, its hold and rapid expansion felt close, humbling, terrifying, and real in those dark burial grounds. Some scholars think that

when Paul wrote his letter to the Romans, in 56 C.E., Christians were a congregation of fewer than 150 in the entire city.

6

Focusing on the spiritual message of the catacombs when I first lived in Rome was like digging in a fallow garden at the end of winter. There is always some reluctance, as well as anticipation, in the act of facing the slow return to life. Descending into the catacombs, a visitor approaches, in a physical way, the mystery of funereal practices: when identity is proclaimed by burial itself, because it takes place among others of the same creed. In these dark rooms and tunnels, Romans hid and also held services of faith. These are facts. People here were feverishly doing something new. Whether or not they died for their beliefs, they lived them in a society that not long before had executed several hundred gladiators in a single afternoon and relished the spilled blood. How many among the early martyrs were fanatics and how many were individuals freed from small images of themselves? That question remains a difficult one to interpret in any period of religious fervor or activism without citing the support of written testimony. So I always imagined the people in these early centuries as seeing their lives as Saint Augustine did his: a self changed by a new inner life. But I knew that it must not have been that way for many. My experiences then were speculative. I resisted what it felt like to have such a certain faith, nor did it much interest me.

7

When I dig in our dormant Parma garden, as the shovel gingerly churns soil, the first signs of life are the sluggish wiggle of worms or the startled eyes of lizards awakened from their winter hibernation. Finding creatures who live underground or who rest there in order to reenter when the earth is warmer, I connect deeply with the idea of preparation, of visiting darkness, the underground, of disturbing dormancy in order to assist the conditions for new spring life. The catacombs were an early manifestation of Christianity that I visited in order to touch one dusty root of what was to come in a religion that spread across the world. Imagining people gathered in those cramped spaces to carry out their burial services recalled for me the strength of others who held on to beliefs and moved from the underground to open, nonviolent resistance—people in Selma, New Delhi—based in part on the strength of those first believers.

Climbing back out of the catacombs, sunlight and wide skies awaited me. Even when clouds covered much of the blue, the energy of the light was impossible to contain. Returning to the light affected me outside Sant'Agnese. My reaction, literal and mundane, was without nuances. It had to do with being young, resisting the complications of religion, the violence and clashes it inspired, feeling judgmental about the Catholic Church's wealth. Embracing sunshine was sheer pleasure. At twenty-six, captivated by philosophies that stressed freedom and free choice, I was still quite far from realizing how and why my quest included God. At the time, buzzing with enthusiasm and energy, merely awakening in the courtyard at first light with carts clattering over the stones at four-thirty or five in the morning provided all the signs of transcendence I needed. Most days, Rome blazed with sun, warmth, simple pleasure on the skin.

V

Light

What light through yonder window breaks?

—Romeo and Juliet

1

Light in Rome is very distinct from light, say, in Venice, or Florence. Its muscular brightness is in part due to its geographical location. In summer, contrary to what one might think, the city's southerly latitude provides it with twenty minutes less of summer light between sunrise and sunset than in Milan. But its position near the sea and its spaces, ruined and vast and pompous, lavish its climate with light that inspires colors to speak: the lemons and oranges found in gardens along the Aventine Hill; the purple bougainvillea that climb to outreach the palms and groaning peach trees. Rome's nearly constant light crisps the sheets and shirts and underwear flapping on lines and drying all over the city. The tattered billows, some sheets faded, threadbare, are in daily harmony with the puff and swell of Baroque monuments. Mediterranean light that produces ripe, colored fruit overflows with extravagant and exotic possibilities: dark eyes, low dresses, gardens and scents, clustered excess to be admired, picked, displayed, eaten, enjoyed.

The light of Rome—caught on buildings that are rounded like cumulus clouds, on white marble that is sometimes black with grit now, or on the reddish brick that composes broken and smoothed-over Roman ruins like the Largo di Torre Argentina—softens and warms any path that can be seen from the seven hills. It turns the bluish copper domes gold or leaves them a dusty blue-silver and meets the reds and oranges, the tarnished marble whites, melting and mixing them in amazing, lingering, and bright embraces.

The light of Rome was entirely new to my northern mind. I

got so that I could read it through the small windows of my two-room house. My eye, used to the bluer light of the Midwest, a gray and lovely light that often had snow in it, and whites that intensified it, could calibrate Rome's yellow light and enjoy its minutes, each one different but also lighter, more extravagant, not precious, just as the lemons and oranges were not precious, because there were so many that they could be left to rot or waste.

Roman light danced in my eyes. It was as if an earlier ancestor who navigated by sight had surfaced within me. Light began to meet the Earth's spinning and it charged a timepiece in my consciousness as accurate as a Rolex calibrated to count seconds. I never wore a watch in Rome. The discovery of a city where sun kept pace with my breath, feeding my spirit with messages of constant light, reoriented not only my idea about beauty but also ideas about how its abundant presence shapes culture and mind. The powerful offerings and demands of sun, of course, included heat. Mind-bending and stultifying in the summer months, it blared and beat one back into staying inside. The volcanic black stones paving the streets were mosaics that also broke this light into fine shapes, as if they were light-catching nets. Around two in the afternoon, when the shops were closed, when waves of heat rose up, the scorching raven black streets of Rome sometimes undulated, flapped, and flew.

2

As a writer, I cannot quite put it into words, but a building in Rome communicates a singular view of ancient light. In the Pantheon, one can feel the spiritual power that existed in imperial Rome and how it differed in spirit from the Christianity that arose from and around it. Supposedly stripped of its bronze external covering by the ambitious Barberini family, who had the precious metal melted for use in Gian Lorenzo Bernini's baldachin in

St. Peter's and to embellish their own palace in the 1600s, the denuded brick dome, as brown as a huge toad, still frames the city's light in its most powerful form. Not a focus for measurement, as were Egyptian temples or Stonehenge, not a scientific peephole on the universe, as telescopes would become, the Pantheon incarnates a direct relationship between human life and the sacred sky. The two continue with an uninterrupted connection. The Pantheon hunches down, in Via della Rotonda, surrounded by traffic and tourists. In part because of its solidity—its height is equal to its width—its massiveness is easy to underestimate. Its thick, unmagical solidity—no flying buttresses, no Baroque twists—makes its authority close to that of seeing unified consciousness embodied.

Hadrian, the visionary emperor and poet, adopted by Trajan as his son, designed the Pantheon as a sanctuary for all gods, a place that would reproduce the terrestrial sphere and the cosmic one. He struggled with nearly insuperable technicalities in order to produce a space embodying the experience of human beings confronted by the sky. Its continuous curved inner space has nothing to do with womblike enclosure. Roman and earthly, adapting the remains of an earlier temple, it works like the huge curve of

a shield or a giant cave. The dome above it, its rounded curve above the round walls, belongs to an emperor's vision. It could be a gigantic cranium protecting the brain. The association between consciousness and the dome as a massive house for consciousness is not forced because of the gigantic eye it contains. Hadrian permanently opened a round eye to the heavens and rimmed it with bronze. Open to dark and light, to gods who preceded his time, gods of chaos and order, trickery and honor, his writing reveals that he had no objection to considering himself one whom the sun followed.

Through this simple and sublime lens, the life-giving light of Rome spills its gold onto the vast circular floor. It beams light at the same time it draws eyes upward to space, where gods reside. In all senses, this insight never closes. At some hours, light travels along the walls. At others, sky simply asserts its presence.

"Other domes and pediments will arise from our domes and pediments." That is what Hadrian envisioned. The ability to glimpse the changes in the heavens in the temple that is reconsecrated as a Catholic church makes it one of the most powerful spaces in Rome. Giving light a central place ensures that this ancient building will always keep its original sacredness. It coexists with and overshadows the Christian images that are introduced, while the originally conceived quadrangles that decorate the dome assert serene, rational order. All in the open, the history and structure of the Pantheon remain a totality too vast to ever be fully experienced. Each visit, though, is a discovery of a few minutes of doubt, when the present world can seem puny and shortsighted.

The scale of the Pantheon's dome and its simplicity, besides striking a precedent for the heights and strengths of other domes that would start to rise in the Renaissance, still communicate a message that is rare in what was built later. Because it's open, it doesn't make height an exercise in contemplation, as in the Gothic; nor does it make intellectual prowess and lavish celebration features of rounded heights, as in the Renaissance. Its raw, forceful mystery penetrates and prevails in an awesome temple that shows all that man can do and know.

By stressing natural forces—rain that enters from the sky and pours into the sanctuary, turning its marble slick and slippery; cold that dusts frosty ice across the walls; or bloodred sunsets that tint the faces of those inside—the windowless stone walls holding up a dome with an aperture offer another way of interpreting light in Rome. Light's peregrinations give us pause. Its strength carries associations from earlier times, when human beings' need to look up, and even to search for malevolent gods, was a given. Uncertainty, danger, not knowing were part of understanding. Emperors fall, but the sun warms or scorches the earth and sustains all life.

The dome's empty eye requires no doctrinal attention. The silence can be visited by anyone who is curious or in a meditative mood, in spite of the Vespas racing around the Pantheon's stones. The blank eye echoes the she-wolf as Rome's first mother. The temple's majesty refuses postmodern interpretations of previously unseen realities that bring forth new ways of seeing what was there. It was and shall be what Hadrian imagined it to be. Its dome

powerfully covers, while showing us how we are forever exposed. Even though the somber temple has been consecrated as Christian, it stands stoic and dominating, outside that message. Above us, not just the sun or winds or night but other perpetual forces move relentlessly beyond our greatest capacities to know them.

VI

Hungry and Untrained Eyes

It is still an open question if we will grow
into Catholics or into Christians.

—Adam Zagajewski, "We Know Everything"
(translated by Renata Gorczynski)

1

In my courtyard, I was only two minutes from the Cancelleria, an imposing Renaissance palace attributed to Bramante and belonging to the Vatican. Amid the clog of carts and temporary market stands, there was a continuous line of diplomatic cars, black shiny Mercedes and Cadillacs, pushing the crowds aside. With a flourish common to official vehicles, national flags fluttered near the rearview mirrors, while security men swished curiosity seekers away. The international aspect of the Catholic Church spilled over daily into the square, bringing costumes, cavalcades, the accoutrements of diplomacy and power. It brought an incredibly strong sense of international government to a place that was ordinarily swamped by iron-wheeled carts from the market and sellers hawking clothes cheaply: Missoni and Etro dresses heaped like so many fallen blossoms. The long arm of the Vatican's presence made an impression, both ritualized and modern, as if a king occupied the Cancelleria. His subjects might gawk, but they never tried to participate. Only Oreste, a tragic man with mental problems who worked in the courtyard, tried to crash the gates. Often, he returned bloodied, perhaps by security men.

This modern, institutional form of the Church as an earthly power added a dimension to all the churches that one wandered into to view a masterpiece, light a candle, or sit. The scope of its kingdom was ever present, far and beyond the single church one chose to enter. Even when you were trying not to hear the noise of coins dropping into the box for alms or the box for making a bulb light up over some treasure, it was hard to avoid contemplating the Church's vast organizational reach.

Like the ancient empire that lasted for centuries by offering citizenship and rights to conquered peoples, in Rome, signs of Catholic cultures and populations expressing something of their different origins were inevitable. Just as one settled in to enter silence, history called, and before you could say "Italian," often the surrounding objects proposed continuity built from the Church's having subdued and then accommodated different cultures. Santa Maria dell'Anima is a German national church begun in 1350, restored and expanded by Bramante, sacked by the French in an eleven-year war, divided up one hundred years later during the Thirty Years' War, before becoming once again a German-language church where Austrians, Germans, bishops and pilgrims and students still find a home. In San Luigi dei Francesi, the Contarelli Chapel with Caravaggio's paintings pulls the visitor in, but soon after, figures in French history—Charlemagne, Clothilde, Joan of Arc—conduct one away from Rome and into another country's relationships to the Church. The long centuries of religious struggle in different countries and empires to establish and consolidate Catholicism mean that, not paradoxically, war and power can feel like celebrations or announcements emerging from darkened chapels. Signs of victories and defeats linger; spoils of war remain on display. Yet in the persistence of coexisting cultures that are incorporated into the institutional church—starting from the bilingual panels translating treasures acquired in this process (Spanish/Italian, French/Italian, Polish/Italian)—the long-term view of Catholicism illustrates inclusion as a process of assimilation leading to peace.

2

In the Vatican, oddly enough, my most frequent stop was at the *Laocoön*, a first-century B.C.E. Hellenistic statue that Julius II

purchased in the sixteenth century, after it was discovered in a garden that was most likely part of a complex belonging to the emperor Titus. So important was the aura around the work (probably
a copy) done by three sculptors from Rhodes that told the tale of
the man punished by Athena for his warning about Greeks bearing gifts to Troy that Rome's people, workers and nobles alike,
were given an official holiday when the statue was installed in
the papal gardens in 1506. The city, sensitized to classical ideals, in
part because of its own existing ruins, celebrated the day in dance
and song, and people feasted on whatever food and wine they
could lay their hands on.

The inclusion of the entire population, both literate and illit-
erate, in the celebration was, in part, the fruit of pre-Gutenberg
times, which for centuries occasioned the visual retelling of stories. Extending to all social classes a sense of identity arising from
art was a development that originated in the diffusion of Christian
stories. The practice of regiving and retelling biblical events
through painting emphasized the importance of art, so that art,
too, became commonplace and integral to all. The celebration
of the discovery and acquisition of the Laocoön implied the broader
importance of the statue that had been found, even if the poorest
soul would probably never see it. The clerk in the police station,
who dictated a paean to Italian culture, knowing it would get me
a work permit, radiated this unbroken inheritance. Art may or
may not be a heartfelt need in citizens' lives, but by belonging to
all, it stimulates encounters with beauty and excellence. All Romans have this pride and respect for work that expresses higher
learning and experience of worlds that are beyond most people's
creative reach. They are comfortable with the notion of genius.

Tourists, too, are able to experience the effects of identification
that patronage brings. It happens all the time in churches. Their
entire contents belong to you for as long as you sit in darkened
space, and then drop the coin, so that the shadows covering
Ghirlandaio's fresco lift their veils. As the money slips from your

fingers, you step into the glow of patronage. You altruistically sponsor the spotlight. It's a pleasurable act, an amazing moment, once you stop grumbling about the Church's propensity to tax. And when the light parsimoniously and cruelly snaps off, just as you have found your focus, the idea of ownership falls back to earth. You join all the others straining their eyes in the dark and wondering how many euros it will take to view the painting as if one were actually a lord.

3

The reason the *Laocoön* was the work I deliberately visited, sometimes giving up on the Sistine Chapel or Rafaello's fresco of the School of Athens, with its sublime space and flanks of notables, if there were big crowds, fits the same pattern that drew me toward many other sites in the city. The inclusion that we all seek, that all human beings seek, was to be found in the Vatican in my Rome years, though not in its own stories, when imagery, centuries of art supporting its views, was too strictly religious or expressions of Church power too ornate. In that massive museum, I liked objects from the classical period, historical maps, and specific works that were passages in art history from one era to another. I operated under a set of restrictions, a pattern of unconscious selection. Discovering this feels like viewing an X-ray that shows us our bones. The certainty of the midwestern point of view of my early Protestant education made the diversity and the multiplicity of images that stood outside of Catholic images the ones that I unconsciously found compelling when I first began to open my hungry and untrained eyes.

Exploring the barriers in upbringings, the weirdness of clashes and stories of oppression and injustice that are inherited as identity, was in some ways fashionable in the late sixties. Racial and religious segregation as well as ethnicity were under scrutiny in order to better understand the social formations that created these seemingly insuperable and, and for that very reason, unexamined borders. Psychoanalysis was often a personal litany of middle-class problems, while the issue of identity as defined by belonging to a country or a social group was not looked at critically as part of that exploration. One was from Northern Ireland, or Naples, or Rhodesia, and each of those labels implied an upbringing that came with the baggage of class, ethnic assumptions, and history. When that aspect of consciousness came around for examination, it was often to tell stories of past injustices or entitlements, rather than to look at the assumptions about the relevance of those categories for identity itself.

In the Rome years, to discover that I was a Protestant—even though I was not actively religious—was to recognize someone who abhorred prejudice and yet had been carefully vaccinated against Catholics and what I had been taught were their false idols and their disregard for truth. In those years, at university it was basically understood that if people of different religions were growing serious about one another, it was a mistake. Seas of tears were shed in our dorms, sincere tears, protective of inherited beliefs. I remember feeling perplexed, saddened, and then incensed about the reality of my own tears when a pensive young man explained it was useless to continue our relationship because he could never marry a woman who was not a Jew.

4

Most people uncover terrible doubts in their lives when they must face loss. When loss appears, issues that were unclear suddenly become the past and are confined among all the possible light and shadows that spring up. How to gauge them, in my experience, is disorienting, as if banks of fog covered and then lifted, weighed down and then moved, leaving uncertainty about where one has been and what one is in. The conflicts intensify if one has left a country, a language, relatives, and the constant framing of what then becomes a receding and often blurred or fossilized past. An acute sense of fragmentation can creep up and grip. Suspended and physically distant, memories can assume so many meanings that may be relevant to identity or may be mere sentimental insistence on stories that are truly lost.

5

I sit in churches in Italy. It is an internal assent. Only recently have I realized that it is quite an act of tolerance on the part of the church that my presence is not questioned once I linger. As a young person who could sit for an hour of silence on a hard bench in a Quaker meeting, I recognize that in dark Italian churches the benches are equally hard. The silence I seek is more or less the same. When I was young, I could not have said this without claiming the differences and distances in our beliefs. Now and then, I don't have quite the detachment in Italian churches that Phillip Larkin conveys in his poem "Church Going." I can't quite claim his ironic read of "the holy end" or his scouring the church for historical treasure, but I recognize his detachment and, at the same time, his being drawn to a space that has been held open for contemplation: "A serious house . . . Which, he once heard, was proper to grow wise in, / If only that so many dead lie round."

Beauty, mysticism, pain are what I experience today when I sit in a church in Italy and slowly quiet my mind. I give up some narrow sense of knowing and lean into a far greater sense of not knowing, a sense of place that goes beyond the physical space around me. I feel the cool air coming off the marble floors. I see islands of electric candles in front of different altars. I hear voices, talking, the tourist guides, and the explosive "Shh" of old women who want quiet. Plaster angels, stucco furbelows, monstrous caskets with marble likenesses of soldiers and ladies: There are few corners left unembellished. I feel something that I resist as temporal, over-blown to the point of being humorous. But then I feel the long, long search and my own knowledge of the spirit and I am grateful to participate in this collective urge that is beyond seeking. I feel space held open, open for centuries, offering the central message of love and institutional custodianship. Yes, I say. Without words, I am carried toward yes.

In the Rome years, I rarely stopped in churches for anything other than visiting art or hearing marvelous free concerts. It was in Venice, before my Italian husband and I married, that I probably first felt the utterly ancient shelter that churches offer. We were caught in the basilica of Santa Maria Assunta to get out of the gale that was sending boats slapping against the docks. I was drip-ping wet: coat, skirt, shoes. My husband-to-be took his soaking in stride. But I was rarely a good sport when wetness chilled me to the bone. He urged me to take off my shoes and socks. I feared it was disrespectful. He removed the day's newspaper, which he had kept inside his jacket. Slowly, with deliberation, he ripped it and formed, as if he had a scissors and a model, two well-shaped soles. He lined my shoes. He removed my socks, rubbed my icy feet, and spread the limp wool on the pew. A twelfth-century mosaic of a large, elongated Mary dressed in deep blue and sunk into a back-ground of gold tesserae glowed in the wide apse above the altar. How could I be removing my shoes and socks in a church? Yet I understood perfectly. My husband felt comfortable seeking shelter and saw no reason not to. What were wet feet to the Church and to the centuries? In the unheated stone place, with undulating mosaic floors fixed like permanent waves, we huddled together, included in the large silent offer to rest. The wind howled outside and whistled under the door. No one else came in.

6

The *Laocoön* in the Vatican Museums is thought to be a copy of a sculpture of the Hellenistic period, from an earlier tradition. It depicts a myth. The marble statue of a father and two small boys, who, like many renditions of children, were not completely convincing, was smaller than I had imagined. I had carried its storied movement in my memory from a university art history class in Ann Arbor, Michigan. Greek art was the apotheosis of technical skill and beauty. As I viewed artworks from slides projected on a large screen, following the progressive development of Western art, the masterpieces had floated, each for the better part of an hour, as giants in the dark.

At first glance, in the Vatican courtyard, the *Laocoön* was not nearly as spectacular as Michelangelo's *David* or Bernini's *Saint Theresa*, which occasioned what in the 1960s was titillating student debate about her ecstasy. That was the time of "Je T'Aime," which had Jane Birkin singing over an orgasm, in spite of the Vatican's censorship. Besides Birkin's, the most popular song in my courtyard, a San Remo winner, insisted on a more proletarian message: "He who doesn't work won't be allowed to make love." Equality for the sexes, as well as the names and sounds of eros, were realities bursting across on sound waves into everyday life, even in my Roman courtyard.

The *Laocoön* was consigned to an out-of-the-way place, where it seemed almost ordinary. But once I got nearer, the Greek statue's image of inescapable, immediate terror impressed me. It was not about the psychology of torture, but that of terror. Questions of morality twisted in the interpretation, which spoke of punishment for betrayal, meted out by a goddess.

The snakes wrap around the three bodies like tightening chains or lashing whips. Their strength (expressed by the undulating way they encircle the figures and by their outsize proportions) introduces an ambiguous relationship with narration because of their sinuous vitality. They add, in spite of their awful nature and task, sensuous and visual elements that are so powerful that one loses, by moments, a resistance to their presence. This contradiction and tension probably are what make the composition so strong. Their knotted and undulating rhythms and the intensity of the struggle fascinate and repulse as they overwhelm their human victims.

The carved moment, the physical pain of the father and sons, carried with it the story of before and after: Athena's decision to punish Laocoön for trying to warn the Trojans about Greeks bearing gifts. The marble, showing only the ultimate event, writhed like a film of the whole story. It alerted me to many issues in the rendering of the Crucifixion of Christ that dominated visual expression of suffering for more than fifteen hundred years. It also struck my rebellious side. Was Laocoön really to be punished for having tried to save a group from war and destruction?

The strategy of narrative in art was a topic suggested and easily analyzed when viewing works of art in Rome. Most figurative art

was never wholly itself, but came accompanied by oral and written versions, not only about context but also about successive actions. A specific moment always narrated the arc of other moments. It was interesting to discover support and scaffolding in sacred stories and myths, and slowly to analyze how modern art, seemingly freed from narrative, actually carried its own myths about fracturing and disjunction into each isolated image. A statue like the *Laocoön* helped me to understand the way Italian painters discovered narration in depicting the Crucifixion episode of Christ's life. Telling the Crucifixion in an image could be done in endless ways, depending at which point you stopped the frame.

The *Laocoön* was fiercely cruel, and its myth, known by the viewers, raised the issue of the meaning in that suffering. The statue of the tormented man and his two sons (who in some way were left to struggle alone) was never just itself. Unsupported by the story, the image might have been bizarre. Instead, the deliberate nature of the snakes' deadly attacks was meant to horrify. The image of physical terror—the result of punishment that also extended to one's family because of an act of political betrayal—was meant to burn in the viewer's memory.

Buttressed by the myth, if you knew it, the meaning could move beyond. When I first saw the suffering in Laocoön's face, I brought to it my ideas about the Vietnam War. The same statue could represent torture in modern situations where dissidents fear their families will be targeted for reprisals. I remember being moved by the depth of the representation. The statue was actually a play that could be reviewed, not only for its technical qualities but also for its multifaceted meanings.

7

The depiction of Mary—a topic that was almost completely suppressed in Protestant thought and history—was not a subject that

I discovered or dwelled on in the Vatican Museums. It was no ideal of mine as a university student looking for images of women as protagonists. Rosina, the crippled and poverty-stricken woman who sat in the window under my apartment, first struck me as a disturbing embodiment of some of the qualities of the sitting figure that I associated with the Madonna. Rosina's mystery set off silent chimes about women and their roles. Her poverty and passivity were far from bra burning and glass ceilings, the liberation battles of those years.

Through Rosina, though, I came to an issue that was of greater urgency and meaning to me. The way she lived embodied the mystery of suffering. Suffering as an existential element, endemic in the human condition, was different from considerations about how to alleviate it. It was a divide, between pragmatic thinking and, perhaps, philosophical thought, that had always appeared difficult to bridge in the years in which I was still studying in Oxford and Michigan.

Rosina's presence at her window is a relevant example of reality that I think the philosopher Giambattista Vico would have called a "torturous twist"; however it was to be addressed, the procedure, involving empathy, would not be found by using narrow logic or the "straight line." Her existence presented a model that fit with religious images as well as with all of the secular premises about life's meaninglessness.

Deep-throated women like Minica, who controlled the courtyard, giving orders, taking messages, determining what actions should be taken even by the men, presented another version of women's role and place. Because she was a woman of action, meaninglessness was never a frame for examining her life. Minica, with her wagging finger, the commander of the yard, who had borne six children, had been arrested and jailed for selling small things like bags of lentils in order to carry her family ahead, was a matron with power. Her husband, who shoveled coal in steam engines and lost his eye when a burning coal escaped, died early. She

took over. No one ignored her gray head. When her bulldog jaw went firm and she clicked her tongue, all courtyard games stopped.

8

In the Rome years, Mary's predecessors were generally those who captured my attention: the she-wolf, the Archaic bodies, the realistic marble busts of Roman women with their stylish hairdos and, eventually, their faces lined with realistic wrinkles. Their recorded and interpreted lives, from that of the empress Livia to those of the early Christians who left sobering notes about the paradise that would be found after the lions had mauled their flesh, were vivid and dramatic. Ancient Rome, in its poets' and historians' accounts, was rife with murders, intrigues, affairs, and divorces leading to unions of love as well as power and martyrdom. Roman men and women were depicted with accuracy and their characteristics seem to have been cloned and copied, passed directly through genes to the handsome, harmonious, and often strong features of contemporary Roman faces encountered at nose length on the city's crowded buses.

The ancient Romans' progressive refinement of representation reflected thinking about truth and an aspiration to create unidealized versions of it. Pictorial realism reached an end point in imperial Rome once Constantine declared Christianity the official religion of the Roman Empire.

The inspiration required to represent the Holy Family became a problem to be faced and understood, since it was ill-adapted to the technical heights of realism, with all its finely depicted wrinkles and irregularities. For more than two hundred years, there was uncertainty caused by the contradiction in depicting entities that had supernatural and nonmaterial qualities. The search for how to depict a Christian God and the Holy Family looked east and west before two versions of Christ began to coalesce. The first standardized icons, the more stylized image, a Christ with almond eyes and dark skin, came from the Middle East. In Russia, the more Western version was found painted on panels made from massive oaks from the Siberian forests. The elaboration of Mary took longer. From a stiff, sexless, meditative figure, she slowly evolved into a human, and even seductive, woman. The Holy Ghost, believed by some scholars to represent the female element in the Trinity, became a dove, or shooting rays of light. And the baby Jesus rarely sheds his look of being a miniature man.

9

Livia, the emperor Ottavian's wife, in the first century c.e., fed her guests in a room saturated with greens and blues depicting palms, cypresses, quince, pomegranates, doves, and laurel. The frescoes, in what is assumed to be her windowless summer dining room, now safely restored and displayed in the National Museum of Rome,

Palazzo Massimo alle Terme, are reframed every hour by a brief change of light imitating the sun's passage during a day. Her garden and the techniques of painting the special details of blue and green leaves and rambling rosebushes are picked up again in the Renaissance, in the scientific observations of Leonardo and the lyrical ones of Botticelli.

When one stands inside this room, with its white doves and its pale, silvery trees, its naturalness brings us close to a feeling of a specific June day. Its slightly faded and occasionally cracked nearly two-thousand-year-old façade, like so much in Rome and the rest of Italy, is in itself a cause for genuine emotion. What elegance, fantasy, and charm were imagined as part of being a good hostess. Her room, discovered in late-nineteenth-century excavations of Ottavian's complexes to the north of the city, is another invitation from the past that extends right up until today in Rome. As in the Sistine Chapel, when Adam's and God's fingers nearly touch, the sense of reaching across time passes from that long-ago place to us. The painters, even in a climate of uncertainty and violence, assumed that they were making beautiful and elegant scenes that would last. The ideas of touching, reaching, inviting, including are embedded in the original conception and act.

When my husband and daughter sat on a stone wall with me in the garden on the Aventine Hill, the orange trees were being exuberantly raided by schoolchildren crowding into them. The trees shook from the roots up. They bent as if in storms. Fruit thumped down like warm hail. As we watched with mock horror, waiting for a whole tree to snap or a child or two to tumble from the branches, I felt the impulse to pick up one of the forgotten treasures. Maybe I wanted to participate in the incredible release of energy. School was out and these young rule breakers were having such fun with freedom. In a matter of seconds, gouging its skin with my fingers, I broke the orange into sections. Then, looking at the orange, vibrant as the persimmons when they were brushed in fast strokes in the *intonaco* on the empress Livia's summer dining

room, I understood its satisfying presence in my hand. The reality of trees laden with fruit in ancient Rome had been encrypted (they assumed forever) by the painter or painters celebrating eating, hospitality, gardens in the empress Livia's dining room. My orange, the persimmons on her walls, the swirl of beauty on that hill were part, each of them, of one point of view. They were in agreement: Life imitated life. And we were here to prove it.

VII

Diamond Fires
and Panting Fountains

Thou shalt remain, in midst of other woe
Than ours, a friend to man . . .
—John Keats, "Ode on a Grecian Urn"

1

The Allies had rushed to it as if to a lighthouse the first night they entered Rome. It was June 4, 1944, and Rome was becoming an open city. The Keats-Shelley Memorial House represented not only a landmark of identity but, more than that, a place of poetry and peace. I often visited the three rooms, a magical shrine that belongs to the world, in my Rome years.

"There was the smell—more of England than of Italy, or so one thinks—of leather bindings that bewitched Henry James. There was quiet, peace, pause." So wrote A. C. Sedgwick of *The New York Times* on the morning after. He and the guard, carrying machine guns, had climbed the steep steps, lighting their way with candles. Alberto Savinio, an Italian writer searching for an image for the harmony of the place, richly lined with books, its wooden paneling and ceilings enclosing memories and remembered lines of poetry, said, "It is like living in a violin." A pamphlet called *A Room in Rome*, written by Vera Cacciatore, reminded me of these facts. Her slim booklet is one that I have reread for forty years. Her close spiritual interpretation of the rooms fit with mine, and if I now borrow from her, it is because she and Keats are indelible parts of me.

Keats's rooms look down on the Spanish Steps. Outside of the museum, Gian Lorenzo Bernini's father's fountain of a sinking boat still shoots out its steady streams. It is impossible not to hear translation that has been rephrased, lightly double-edged, in its falling sounds: "Heard melodies are sweet, / but those unheard / Are sweeter." Keats, Shelley, and Byron tied their destinies inextricably to Italy. They grafted onto their artistic identities a classical world that extended time and included history of rises and falls, grandeur and heroism, without incorporating the middle-class detail that would come to inhabit the art of their soon-to-follow English compatriots, the Victorians.

When I visited the American Express office, which in the late sixties was a booming hub near the Spanish Steps, I heard the same broad fountain splashing that Keats heard, day or night, as he pulled himself to the window. Like him, I was hungry for home. Letters to Americans abroad were often addressed to that office, where on any morning up to a hundred travelers milled around, exchanging stories. As I chatted, I often felt as if I were part of an exciting film—not a bystander in one of Fellini's extravaganzas about ancient or present-day Rome, but, improbably, a character in one of Antonioni's movies, which were as geometric as works by Piero della Francesca, and as enigmatic as one of his favorite actresses, Monica Vitti.

The marble boat fountain teases passersby. It lists as water slowly springs from its bow and prow. Like many Baroque gestures,

Bernini the elder's fountain is an event under way, a wreck in slow motion. The father of the famous sculptor supposedly was called by Pope Urban Vlll to imitate a boat that had washed up on the banks of the Tiber. With irony, he emphasized the entropy of a period when this Barbarini Pope was running up the debt of the Church and using Gian Lorenzo Bernini, the sculptor we know, to take motion to new heights. Like Keats's Grecian urn, the *Barcaccia* stops time. It will never sink. Unlike Keats's urn, however, there is no pathos generated by contemplating the boat's fate. The interpretation of the subject is nearly the opposite: *Things fall apart. There is ruin. So what! Let's make the best of it. It will take ages before the boat touches bottom.* It was one more project of art paid for by power and inspired by reality.

2

I read a lot in my Rome years, trying to match the city's layers to events. I read British authors from Gibbon (noting he made an emotional conversion to Catholicism and was guided by his father back into Protestantism) to Trevelyan and Mack Smith, but I was trying out Verga, Deledda, and Manzoni, in Italian, too. Some lovely British friends had taken me under their wing and fed me writers like Verga. Their library had belonged, in large part, to Percy Lubbock, a literary critic and their relative.

Their library was rich and varied and always generously offered. I read local reports about the desperate, bucolic Rome to which Keats came, a Rome feverish with malaria, where cows grazed near the Spanish Steps, where ruins were muddy, broken reminders of barbarian invasions. Most people had little to eat. Many shared hovels. It seems that then, too, most Romans were known as good and warm people. The urge toward unification was circulating, and around that time there were rebellions against local governments all over the peninsula.

3

The rooms memorializing Keats and Shelley, off to the right side
of the Spanish Steps, conveyed a peace that had its origins in
poetry, outside of time, in the imagination. Without fully understanding why—except that I, too, was prone to deep flights of
imagination in pursuit of an identity that often seemed most
suited to passivity—Keats's rooms and his tender age at death drew
me into a deep identification with the space. I joined many other
people, with rucksacks and sandals, carrying small leather volumes of his poems, who lingered over the letters in glass cases, absorbing and responding to the entirely sweet, lonely, and fated
atmosphere of the rooms. After paying a minimal ticket and leaving a signature on the page opened that day to record visitors'
comments, one joined him, his letters and thoughts. "When I am
in a room with People, if ever I am free from speculating on cre-
ations of my own brain, then not myself goes home to myself: but
the identity of every one in the room begins to press upon me that
I am in a very little time annihilated—not only among Men; it
would be the same in a Nursery of children." The waterlike capacity he had to be annihilated by empathy is undoubtedly why the
rooms seem poignant and intense.

His legacy, his meager estate from the sale of books published
and unpublished, his wish that none of Fanny Brawne's letters
should be given to him to read, so great was his longing for her,
gave evidence of his sensitive humility and the tragedy of his pre-
mature departure. Yet those things alone might not explain the
unique attraction of the rooms. The museum is a very special place,
so different from shrines in Rome where saints' leathery bodies
float under spotlights, or their severed or snatched bones can be
viewed through small glass openings in elaborate gold caskets. This
museum offers the same reflective capacity for others that the poet
had in life. The quiet consciousness of his imminent death can be
found in his last words to his friend Joseph Severn: "Severn—I—

lift me up—I am dying—I shall die easy—don't be frightened—be firm, and thank God it has come." Keats leaves this mysterious sense of calm in the rooms, or so it seemed to me as a young woman. Death was addressed and not hidden away in a sad, immobile silence. It was unmistakably present, neither celestial nor an end to be feared.

4

The four odes Keats had written in England play into his inexorable transformation in Rome. He writes no more poetry once he arrives. The words he had already written and his life in those last few months seem to seep into him, mixing together. He becomes the one dissolving on the night, "half in love with easeful Death," and flowers, the wooden ones in the ceiling above him and those painted on the walls, begin to grow over him. He, underneath, becomes "a sod."

Keats tells Joseph Severn of that very sensation about flowers while he was in Rome, and says that in almost every period of his life, his greatest pleasure had been in watching the growth of flowers and trees. Vera Cacciatore first sent me to this text about the flowers. As Keats nears death, the loss of one form of life also is freeing: "the poet has none—no identity." ". . . when I close / These lids, I see far fiercer brilliances, — / Skies full of splendid moons, and shooting stars, / And spouting exhalations, diamond fires, / And panting fountains quivering with deep glows!" He begins to flow away from the name pressed into his body. He accepts both annihilation and a union with eternity.

The rooms contain that, perhaps because we read so much into them. But Keats's life reveals the sublime effects of poetry. He reaches a state where life extends beyond self or art. Keats also imprints his Rome with faith that does not belong to a church or a specific country but fuses a sublime spirit of poetry with life.

Leigh Hunt says the rooms bring together "all who are of one ac-
cord in mind and heart . . . Christian or Infidel . . . face to face . . .
we are coming after him." The voice being followed is one freed
from any authority except experience.

5

Keats's "Ode on a Grecian Urn" was once known by nearly anyone
who was an educated English reader. In the present world, which
has certainly seen enough death, dying young signifies war, high-
speed crashes, overdoses, AIDS. Students might find it tame to
hear the tale of a young man dying young who lived even love
largely in his imagination. His work might soon disillusion the
reader as too plain for his taste. Melancholy, Sleep, Autumn, and
Nightingales. What kind of plots for suspense do those deep gyres
offer?

6

Scholars have suggested that the "Ode on a Grecian Urn," completed in 1819, was inspired in part by Britain's exposition of the
Elgin marbles, acquired in the period when empire building stimulated appropriation and thinly disguised paternalism. Lord Elgin
rationalized the rightness of shipping the fragments to the British Museum with the justification that the British were rescuing
them from destruction. Keats's ode, if it was stimulated by this
exposition, sidesteps completely this aspect of preservation and
politics.

    Keats's ode, on the suspension of time in scenes on an urn that
continues to express life, emotion, and a civilization, ends with a
couplet that is almost as famous as Hamlet's. "Beauty is truth, truth
beauty":

When old age shall this generation waste,
Thou shalt remain, in midst of other woe
Than ours, a friend to man, to whom thou say'st,
"Beauty is truth, truth beauty,"—that is all
Ye know on earth, and all ye need to know.

This tautology has been repeated, condemned, explicated, and debated since 1820, when he published the ode. There are questions about the punctuation, questions about the object of the address in the last line—who is speaking, the urn, the poet? What is the substance and tone of those observations? Within them there is a suggestion that both beauty and truth might be commodities. But they might also contain the ideals of civilization, or even bear the interpretation that art survives not to inspire humanity but to instruct. The urn, because it suspends time, reminds all who are aware of life's finiteness that being alive is beauty and that this is the only truth we need to discover.

Keats can't tell us what he meant, but the words glitter with movement that finally, like water, can be deciphered only as ripples. Beauty slides by, as always, an uncatchable fish. On the urn are narrations of love, of music, of the religious sacrifice of a garlanded heifer lowing at the skies. While the village is now unknown, the town silent, the rituals lost, the lovers long dead, the pastoral on the urn cannot change: Its trees will never be bare; the lover's kisses will never reach warm lips. The longevity of the physical, or real, urn, its survival for dozens of centuries, however, is a vindication of the purpose beyond its pictorial narration. It survived in part because it was seen as worth saving: a precious container of aspirations meant to run parallel to life. Embedded in the delicate narrations of the figures is the Greek ideal of beauty, which continues to speak to other civilizations and other times. The hard work comes in understanding that beauty is equated with substance and truth, with intelligence. The urn was meant to be a meditation on the value of works presenting, in stories, the importance of life.

7

While T. S. Eliot asserted that the last two lines ruined Keats's poem, I continue to linger on them in light of life in Italy. Permanence in objects provokes many kinds of thinking. Keats's last four odes run through many levels of classical art as he faces the dark shadow of imminent death crossing his young life. The brave feeling he conveys in the urn that life is beauty, life is truth, even when it leaves a heart "high-sorrowful," creates solace that may be overblown but nonetheless occupies space in life's silence. The intensity of gazing on early times and holding their contradictions, admitting the absolute invisibility of those times, is useful in contemplating one's own apparent purpose. The past, in many senses, does not die.

The luscious language in Keats's four odes—their sensuous

melancholy, the piercing sound of the nightingale, the beautiful earth of the senses that will cease to be, the autumn beseeched not to ask about the songs of spring ("Think not of them, thou hast thy music too")—are pressed like wine from the beauty in the reality pondered by the young, dying Keats, who left his surgeon's practice to write. It is as if his life in poetry tries to bring beauty and truth—the beauty of life and the truth of death—into an inextricable and ultimately insoluble bond.

After a debilitating two-month journey by sea to Naples and then by carriage to reach the Eternal City, Keats settles in his three rooms near the Spanish Steps, hoping to regain the strength to fight his tuberculosis. In the classical setting that Rome embodies, Keats touches a world larger than his English one. Although he is transient in all senses, he has placed himself in light that will not fade. Through the gull-filled skies of November 1820 to February 1821, when he dies, he looks out on the Spanish Steps from his bed, pressed down by a low wooden ceiling and limited by narrow windows, without any view of the Tiber, only the obsessive fountain outside. He embarked on a journey where he hoped that the climate might help ("There is no doubt that an English winter would put an end to me"), but also where so many rest, where death has made "one with Nature: there is heard / His voice in all her music." In Rome, it is as if he moves more closely into the worlds he prefigured in the odes. He has reached the land of earlier gods and goddesses, Psyche, the Muses, the waters of Lethe, the glades and thickets, violets and dusk roses, the murmurous haunt of flies. His odes are the charmed magic casements opening on the foam of perilous seas in faery lands. Sick for home, Keats comes to spend his last days just two floors up from the right-hand corner of the Spanish Steps, now so crowded with tours that it is difficult to imagine him looking down and finding solace. Yet the earlier beauty is present, in the fountain where water still sounds, in the pilgrims who journey to see the rooms, in words, found in the little glass cases and in reverberations of interior thought.

8

"Here lies one whose name is writ in water." This was the epitaph Keats instructed Leigh Hunt to place on the gravestone that rests in the modest and slightly pastoral English cemetery in Rome. The quiet of the place is like an English country churchyard.

Beauty and truth, like water itself, assume many colorings and meanings. Human feeling, youth and its intensity gather in what Keats left. His epitaph adds, it seems to me, to the understanding of what he discovered in the annihilation of time, its flow beyond all resolution: light that is never merely the cold light of infinity, but the warmer yellow light of meaning carried and created by perceiving the forward flow of time. He joins real time in order to dissolve. That is ultimately why he breaks our hearts. He lets himself be drowned by dimensions apparent and beloved in everyday life. He writes his farewell letters.

9

In my Rome days, I visited Keats's small bedroom and looked at his death mask and that of Shelley. The connection between work that I had studied and knew by heart and the reality of the rooms where this young, life-loving man faced his death touched me beyond words. I still had not found the means to mourn my father's death. In those rooms, where Keats's death was still remembered by calling up his life, nothing was hidden or shut down. Death had peaceful doors that could be swung open in order to make reference to what had been lived. It was still acceptable to return to his death, his loss, our loss, its mystery.

Sylvia Plath was dead when I first reached Keats's rooms. I didn't know what to make of the numb bitterness and hellish rage that she expressed. The flavor of her imagery was a defiance differ-ent from that of the French Symbolists and yet, like their rebellions, it confirmed extraordinary incendiary capacities in language. The way her poems skimmed reality, scraping its essences, until all blood had been let and the body was drained, lent them an extra aura of truth. Plath's transgressiveness, linked with the result of her irreversible decision, made her poems tragic, not necessarily because of the language but because they document a suicide.

Far more timid souls, less damaged and less hubristic, were in awe of the betrayal she gave voice to. Because she died, her action reinforced the tragic potential of the oppressive reality that composed women's lives. The way creative and academic women lived as second-class citizens meant that she cast an all too lucid light on a dark, unjust place of discontent that middle-class women had said little about. I still was trying to interpret the meaning and indeed discern if there was such a thing as a woman's voice when the startling conclusion to her words was revealed. Something in me reverberated deeply to her images of words as riderless. I feared those images.

Plath, far more than Woolf, was captive to madness as her subject, and by being so, she inadvertently left a bomb site for female writers to sift through. Her dramatic tone and the scatter of rubble she left cast tragic truths on the reality of being split. She was a woman trapped in her generation; she had been wounded not only by society's assumptions but also by her own sense of abandonment after her father's death. Plath could not sort out the deceit that words carry even though they seemed to mirror perfectly the deceits of her life. Her voice breached the most terrifying taboos. Inside of poetry's chambers, at first the words blazed; then she started to crawl and could not get out of the exploding fire.

Keats outstared madness and followed his knowledge of death to another extreme, another form of annihilation. His conclusion was nothing he worked at. It was his nature. "If a sparrow come before my Window I take part in its existence and pick about the Gravel." In spite of my bravado and the bold side of my personality that often expressed feelings that could find echoes in Plath's rage (especially about losing her father), I held close his vision of serenity in tragedy.

In Rome, countless times his experience pointed me back to the courtyard, to the passivity and mystery of Rosina, to the need to find words in Rome that fit with my own watery propensity for empathy and my need to construct a female body and voice that moved beyond a deep distrust of words' capacity to distort. "Don't be frightened," in many different ways, became a mantra. Keats's belief in "Negative Capability"—"being in uncertainties, Mysteries, doubts, without any irritable reaching after fact & reason"— offered brotherly comfort. Peace, which he obtained, was something I sought.

VIII

The Square

You live here? Oh my God, I'd give anything to be able to do that.

—woman in an elevator in Milan

1

Age, in Italy, is not a metaphor. It breathes, in cities, often under bright skies, sometimes laboring with stale breath. The cathedral and the municipal palace—that arresting arrangement of power through the ages, the extravagance of the ongoing architectural language, the decoration, the improvements, the weight of the stones with which they have been built, the distances they traveled, the surfaces buffed and cleaned of the centuries that darkened them with soot, with fire, with carbon fumes, the stones, the human labor of erecting them, hundreds of men and often as many years—those two edifices holding watch on a vision of society in each city and often composing the main square, were agreed upon as off-limits by the Allies and the newly formed Italian government under Badoglio in mid-1943. These sites, which had housed government in its two historical forms over centuries, were places that could not be bombed as the Allies started to take Italy back. These squares were visible to planes on the Axis side, as well. In the crosshairs delineating targets, the monuments loomed. They were not strategic like railroad lines or bridges and, also unlike those sites, such buildings were to be destroyed only as a last resort, because they represented civilization and a kind of duration that was frightening to imagine pulverizing.

These special monuments and places were to stand because they had stood through dark periods of bestiality, and it was important that once World War II was over, they remained to be dedicated again to better things. To destroy the historic squares was to commit a crime different from the desecration of human life. It was a murder of centuries of identity, centuries of aspirations that were beyond any single event or memory, beyond any atrocity. Italy lost few of the squares that held the central cathedral or municipal palace, and most of these were accidents—often a corner hit and then fire, since aerial bombs were difficult to direct. Monte Cassino, a monastery eighty miles southeast of Rome, founded by Saint Benedict in the sixth century, was deliberately bombed in 1944 by the Allies, who had been in communication with the Vatican, with the mistaken perception that the Germans surrounding the hill would be driven out.

Ironically, this was the worst destruction among significant monuments that occurred during the drive to take back Italy from the Axis powers. The Germans had decided not to occupy the abbey precisely because they hoped to leave it outside of the raging battle. In a strange note, the abbey, among its centuries of treasures, was holding the documents of the Keats-Shelley Memorial House, which had been sent to them for safekeeping in 1942. The documents were sent by the abbot to the Vatican for safekeeping before the abbey was bombed.

2

The piazza, the Italian square, cannot be taken from anyone who lives here. It stands for a thousand things. The church built of stone can be an object of political resistance: It can be reviled, it can be held sacred, but it belongs to everyone who passes it, both those who cross themselves and genuflect and those who stop merely to study the scaffolding covering the Romanesque sculptures. The square, made of stones and polished by moonlight, lies at the heart of any definition of beauty in Italy. It evokes emotion that seems almost too obvious to notice. It can withstand any sort of diatribe or interpretation and it stays, silent, undeterred. Its effect cannot be put into words—not one person's words, not one century's words.

Squares, because of their duration—every stone worn by sorrow, hope, treachery, intrigue, little hoops rolled past by children, sober horses pulling hearses, soldiers on foot, women, barefoot, singing—because of how the stones have faced all these dramas and tableaux, almost suggest the act of witnessing. The stones stand day and night, keeping watch as well as being seen. They organize deep certainties in an Italian's life, although no one would agree on what those certainties mean. Squares, in the way they fill and empty, the way they hold and brim with some irreducible truth, invite permanent meditation. The ultimate consideration is not history, philosophy, Charlemagne, Mussolini; not Plato, Vico, the labor unions, or soccer. Squares concentrate attention and cancel all white noise. Beauty is the conclusion, the result, the realization of acceptance and calm that emerges from them. Across many centuries, they condition the whole, providing a permanent message of another ungraspable thing—endurance. The square lasts because it embodies the ideals of spiritual and temporal order and

exacts fidelity as tribute from all individuals, who, in turn, perceive its space as a communal offering.

3

The basic and inevitable injunction in Italy to remember time in all its dimensions—its sensations, its history, its futility, the unavoidable reality of age and aging—is what makes the woman riding in an elevator with me blurt out as we lurch toward our respective floors in a Milan airport hotel, "You live here? Oh my God, I'd give anything to be able to do that." I nod, not tempted in any way to deprive her of that feeling for which Italy has sacrificed so much: a feeling of inclusion, continuity, century after century, the presence of time and precedent as a scale for the individual. This view of time as a continuous presence causes little sense of anguish. It holds off all that is banal and temporary.

The Italian relics, ruins, and restored palazzi form the center of most of its major cities as well as most of its tiny villages. These physical realities are the equivalent of having elders. The early monuments are not abstractions. They do not pay nostalgic lip

service to something that has been wiped out. Local governments and foundations have spent inestimable amounts of money to keep them repaired and vibrant. They stand firmly in space, chambers that reverberate with demands.

Human beings, not just in Italy, have benefited from Roman urban planning, rational and efficient, and its extension and modification for the construction of churches, government halls, water systems, and roads. This rich model has filtered down as a general one and as such has no counterpart in the Protestant urban response of later centuries.

Jagged, sublime feats of imagination and engineering purposefully proclaiming new ways to express human commerce and progress have led to different solutions and ideals. Empty vertical space often invites the upward thrust of modern buildings that proclaim what change has surpassed, what progress has discovered and profit allows. These heights contain novelty that is not neutral. They contrast with the now modest height of the brick campanile and seem to boast that the model is quaint and obsolete. Skyscrapers, first of iron and then of steel and reinforced concrete, suggest power shorn of symbols. There is only that message of a single direction—onward, upward, new. Italy, by resisting this approach, has remained committed to squares, the scale of them, and their importance in the shrinking public, shared space of modern life.

It takes believers in memory, in age, to propose a dark shadow side to progress, a cycle that brings it back to other perspectives. A celebration of progress tends to take the rosy, exciting, short view. Instead, shadows and cracks can never be eliminated when age is part of the model. Shadows and cracks are something Italians expect. They expect them in what needs to last. They also anticipate them as reactions to such constant, unchanging ideal standards. This capacity to expect the latter kind of cracks (a concept of lapse) in order to deal with cracks of age is a cultural observation. In its less glorious forms, it allows for the country's propensity for shutting its eyes. It accommodates a placating realism that offers amnesty when too many eyesores have arisen illegally and no one wants to knock them down. It avoids addressing dragging feet. Nor does it judge negatively the frenetic impulse to fill in lips and breasts with silicone and cover bald heads with stitched-in clumps of hair in an effort to stave off age as a destructive force.

IX

Elders

Where was he going and what did he believe?

—comment on Ötzi, the five-thousand-year-old man

found near Bolzano

1

The hundred-year-old man had no hoary beard. His white hair was crisply snipped; his glasses made his eyes seem large and dreamy. He was as neat as a violin's bow, thin, springy on his feet. Born in 1909 near Turin, he was celebrating his centennial in Parma, where some of his siblings (also bright-eyed and with red cheeks) and his son and his son's wife, as well as their son and his wife and child, gathered around him. Snatches of Verdi, courtesy of two overly miked locals; the meal of ham and cheese, tortelli and cappelletti came out on groaning platters for three hours. He made the rounds of the tables, sometimes pausing to see if he could place the faces in front of him. Sometimes he could not, but he knew they belonged in his story, so he waved a hand in the mildest of shrugs, raised his cane, and moved on. The length of time in that golden number *cento*, what takes place in that many minutes, could not be deduced from his motions, which still had strength and purpose. His mind still followed the larger shapes of current events, still formed letters on a page. The technological thread from horses to computers, phonographs to radios, the Spanish flu to the polio injection, rubber to plastic was part of it, as were his great-granddaughter and the long-dead hunting dog, and the clear-sighted decision to leave his job when he was asked to pledge allegiance to Mussolini.

The hundred-year-old man was born into Italy when Vittorio Emanuele III was king. His father taught the king fencing. One of five children, three of whom survive in good health, he was too

young to serve in the first war and too old to be sent to the front
for the second. Graduated as a chemist, he directed a rubber fac-
tory for the war effort in World War II and lost his position when
he refused to join the Fascist Party. He continued to work on the
properties of rubber, performing experiments clandestinely. After
the war, when the country wrote a new constitution and eliminated its king, he applied to use his discovery. Before, in the years
of hunger, and the bombings, and the Fascist and partisan execu-
tions carried out by improvised firing squads in Milan, after Mussolini set up his government in exile in Salò, the hundred-year-old
man took to the woods at night in the dark days of the new moon
or the last of the old to hunt game for his family. Undercover, he
brought home rabbits, pheasants, and smaller birds.

In his early life, he walked. His parents took the family into
the mountains around Turin and he walked often for whole days.
Early on, he found that pace, of breathing and walking steadily.
Walking is something deep in him that has never left his brain
and body. It is deep in the memory of many Italians, deep in their
love of mountains: pairs of boots made from leather and softened
by years of use and special grease; crampons and ropes for the
climbers. More than 320 people living in Milan today, in what are
considered unhealthy levels of pollution, are over one hundred years
old. Most walked and walked as children. Rita Levi-Montalcini, a
student of Natalia Ginzburg's father and a Nobel Prize winner still
doing research, has reached 101. She, too, grew up knowing the
mountains of Turin.

Natalia Ginzburg, in her novelistic autobiography, *Family Say-
ings*, tells many stories of her father's relationship to the mountains, walking and skiing, and she doesn't shy away from slipping
in hers. "So there we went, with hobnailed boots, stiff and heavy
as lead, thick socks and woollen caps, dark glasses on our noses
and the vertical sun beating on our sweating heads . . ." The
regimen—the mixture of pain and pleasure, the focus on health,
on character formation, on childhood as a set of adventures where

movement was equated with regimented freedom—leaps from
memories of Italian childhoods spent summering in the mountains; fresh milk carried home in pails and boiled; dark cliffs; the
sense of destination and arrival as rewarding scenes from the top
of a peak.

The hundred-year-old man also walked in the mountains that
Dino Buzzati wrote about and illustrated in books. These are the
coral-pink mountains where, in *The Tartar Steppe*, the imaginary
Fort Bastiani drew Drogo into the enchantment of waiting and
the hypnotic lure of the void. The Dolomite formations have been
given world protection status by UNESCO, and tourists flock in
for "creamy polenta" and whatever fast takes on eternity have
been packaged by guides.

2

The hundred-year-old man walked every year of his life except for
the first one. He knows the salubrious effects of days and even
weeks or a month in summer spent taking on Apennine paths and
gaining a perspective that mountains bring to a life. He never expressed the moods that Natalia Ginzburg recalls, and that I, as a
very late comer to the experience of seeing a mountain and grasp-
ing its scale, also recognize. It's a feeling of being herded into and
marched toward a goal, and wishing most of the way (although I
know the view at the top will be gripping and even freeing) that
the top was not a goal at all.

The discipline of putting one foot after another for hours at
a stretch inevitably finds a rhythm that is close to a march. Of
course, it expands into many motives and experiences: the beauty
of clean air, the striking and dramatic variety of landscapes in
mountain ranges of the southern Alps, the Apennines and the
Dolomites, which were formed by different geological events. Often there are recent traces of human history. In some areas, one

crosses battlegrounds. In the Dolomites, the horrors of World War I echo in the sheer rock faces that were believed to be strategically useful as Italians and Austrians blindly fought along the mountain ranges for national borders. In one day—April 18, 1917—six thousand Italians and two thousand Austrians died in explosions and avalanches that were part of a campaign that lasted two years. The Italians alone lost over half a million men in the four-year struggle that now is remembered as a victory once they regained control after losing at Caporetto.

The wider time scales fused into the ranges of the Apennines and Alps suggest dramatic symphonies from major stages of the Earth's history. The geological mantles envelop and dwarf the melancholy of the sober war cemeteries, with their thousands of identical white markers. The mountains' grandeur, though, can't be set against the feeling of awe for a single man, our chemist in Parma, who has lived one hundred years. In their complexity and challenge, mountains can only hold out remote volcanic and glacial responses. They invite all to transverse endless paths that are just that: sublime, without visible end. Mountains and the sea are time's perimeters on this peninsula. They are far too old to allude to any close human sadness or joy.

The vitality of the hundred-year-old man excites us because he embodies a victory on a human scale. He is not perfect, but he is not shut away. His professor son still takes him out and fusses over him. They drink coffee in a shopping center, even though he may not quite know where he is. Confusion and spotty memory are expected and tolerated because his body still holds space and his eyes still shine with selective recognition of certain events. A coffee, a shopping center: One has an exotic aroma still steaming from childhood and the other is quite new and its scents stale and unfamiliar. But hand him a chestnut or an olive and he will remember stories. They are objects that do not change and, not just now, they hold dimensions that no one else can see. That is the real mystery. Everyone knows olives, sees chestnuts, picks them up or eats them, and yet his stories are his own. No one will ever again be this hundred-year-old man. Nor will his guests ever see a party like the one going on, with Verdi growing louder by the minute.

3

Most regions in Italy have been walked for millennia. Walking is a national pastime, once obligatory and now recreational, that has made people sturdy and tolerant, patient and rather fearless, at least up until now. Now this long-distance activity is shrinking to a limited population, consisting in large part of pilgrims still following the Via Francigena all the way to Rome. The few Sardinian shepherds who guide their flocks along the riverbeds, their sheep starting at the Tiber and grazing alongside the mouth of the Arno and banks of the Po until they reach cool pastures in the Apennines, are tiny vestiges of the migrations that have occurred each summer and winter since Mesolithic times. The occasional large flocks of long-legged sheep that reach the north now appear like enchanting low clouds on the green fields they pass through.

The thought of long-distance walking brings back an earlier traveler, Ötzi, found on the border in the Ötztal Alps between Austria and Italy when the ice that had preserved him began to melt and he was released from the spot where he died, facedown, five thousand years ago. There he was, in 1991, a long-distance walker, uncovered nearly whole. His shoes were a wonder of bear-skin soles, deer-hide lasts, a net of tree bark, and he wore grass socks. His feet were better equipped to walk and survive the cold than those of the soldiers in World War I who froze in Dolomite caves. He wore a hutlike cloak of grass, which covered his leather clothing.

The various kinds of wood from which his seventeen arrows were made express the rich vegetation of the time: yew, viburnum, dogwood, willow, birch, chestnut, beech. Red berries and two kinds of mushrooms remained in his pouch with its scraper and drill and awl. What do these beautiful objects say about forests, about hunting, mountains, countries, about culture and taboos? He had a few tattoos and an arrowhead in his shoulder. Where was he going and what did he believe? He fell in the mountains at around an age that was less than half that of the hundred-year-old man. Ötzi was young enough to be the hundred-year-old's grandson, if we are

willing to overlook the stretch of fifty centuries during which
he was frozen.

4

Once the hundred-year-old man had the chance and luxury to
learn how to downhill ski, he took up winter life in his fifties, so
that he could zoom through the mountains, enjoying a different
speed and balance. He wore a ski hat of bright colors that fitted
close to his head. He read manuals to learn the theory of skiing, as
he had read scientific manuals when he studied chemistry. He
skied into his early nineties, with a determination that got him
up early each morning to eat a large breakfast of milk, coffee, and
bread, always at the same hour. Born when heat was something
generated by the body—by moving, by eating to keep warm—he
kept regular hours. Those hours marked deadlines that creased
him with anger if they were not respected. An intellect who refused to be bored, with a self-sufficient superiority that honored
simplicity, he knew how to give orders about what he needed. He
often kept silent, however, proudly or even wisely, unwilling to
express what his thoughts were.

I've eaten across the table from him many times, when we dine
with his son and daughter-in-law. He cuts food neatly, and eats
neatly. He listens, although I know from our friends that he is hard
of hearing and proud, so some of the silence is appearance. At
Christmas, other friends also joined for a meal, and they had parents ages ninety-five and ninety-seven. It is difficult not to be fascinated by very old people who, while not fully lucid or functional,
have not been cut out of the flow of daily life. They react defiantly
to the fierce way life is taken away. Gratitude is usually not one of
their moods. Their children, who are grandparents themselves,
are often worn thin by a value considered an ancient and basic
truth. They make sacrifices to honor a cycle that starts with de-

pendency at birth and ends with it at death. The responsibility can distort their own lives and freedom, dominate certain choices, and yet not to fulfill it would deprive them of a sense of who they are.

Old age does not hide in Italy. Even if one is lucky enough to reach it, the reality holds compromises and fears, but it will not be erased or concealed. Dust is always being swept up in the piazzas, and the old people sitting in them, with their canes and floppy hats, hold permanent places at the café tables, even when they are a little muddled or idly drinking. Dust, an obsession—surfaces in houses are rubbed over and over until they shine—is a biblical metaphor for life's beginning and end. It conforms to how the Italian family cycle is defined.

5

Today each line I write about this man pulls me in many directions. Writing about elders and how they are part of the family opens up the truth about a way of life aspired to in Italy, and brings up the American model. My mother, at ninety-five, lives in a comfortable residence and lives out a set of expectations that is entirely different for her and for her four children. Except for my younger brother, who resides nearby, we have no immediate responsibility for her. The feelings of closeness, weight and satisfaction, burdens and frustration are not there in any immediate or abundant way. We are not richer for that loss of connection; physically, we separated long ago.

How to suggest the effects of the personal partially shaped by a culture is what I am after. Basically, it boils down to a dream I had last night, where golden pollen spilled and dusted itself over everything—faces, roads—and left large shifting surfaces of pollen that seemed to be trusted with the work of spreading change. Life is perpetuated by breeding, by relationships, by attraction, by supporting dialogue. The discourse on the meaning of culture, on terms like *human rights*, on the political importance of Futurism, on robots, on workers' conditions, on pacifism remains a constant in a country that believes that history and age hold an important place. Society changes. Words are refilled, spilled, and insisted upon as elements to add to common understanding. But the attraction of words—their fertile loads, their specific possibilities to re-create life, to convey emotions—that golden richness fascinates, and it was present in the dream. Everything was sleeping under the pollen. Excessive, wasted, covering and yet being blown away, each grain was part of necessary cycles. While fertilizing the next generation, pollen communicated the mystery of life. "Beyond you" and "bigger than you," nothing lives without what comes from before. How elders are perceived, and how they see themselves, are surely latent meanings in the dream, in that phase when pollen spreads on the ground, covering and yet remaining largely unused. It's excessive, redundant, but each grain contains the need to perpetuate itself.

Pollen. Golden. Part of family. Resonant. Striving.

Blown away.

Wasted.

I awoke feeling anguished. It was as if the dream were referring to my relationship to my mother; how much she had passed on, in spite of all that had been lost or unused.

X

Il Condono

A talent is formed in stillness, a character in the world's torrent.

—Johann Wolfgang von Goethe, *Torquato Tasso*

1

Il condono is perhaps one of the most pragmatic and extensive of Italian solutions for certain kinds of wrongdoing. Wait long enough and, common lore says, the penalty will be reduced or eliminated, for both tax and construction offenses. The price of coming forward can actually be less than if the offender had never broken the law. An example would be the last window for bringing back offshore accounts, when instead of applying the progressive tax schedule of up to 50 percent that would have been applied had the money never left the country, a modest 5 percent was charged, thus rewarding the lawbreaker with inestimable gains on all those illegal years.

Misappropriating money is held to be a lesser act of wrongdoing. Giulio Andreotti, a man who was prime minister seven times, in a trial in Perugia that accused him of ordering the murder of a journalist, Mino Pecorelli (he was found not guilty), remarked about his men, who were accused of laundering money: "They were not criminals. Their crimes were basically economic ones."

Although the statement "The Law Is Equal for All" is appended in Italian courtrooms, a widespread public attitude holds that, at best, this is only an aspiration. Trials to examine the wrongdoing of politicians while they are still in office were put beyond reach under the previous prime minister, Silvio Berlusconi, who passed a law to that effect. The investigations of his possible criminal activities thus postponed, his permanent retinue of forty lawyers knew that his alarming number of pending trials would slowly slip beyond the statute of limitations. Even were he found to be guilty, most sentences would be a virtual slap on the wrist.

A major trial held in Palermo beginning in 1996 and ending in 1999 charged Giulio Andreotti with collusion with the Mafia. Acquitted after three years in a courtroom inside the Ucciardone Prison in Palermo, which had been built to accommodate thirty iron cages for witnesses in the Mafia maxitrials of the 1980s, Andreotti made a characteristically sibylline statement about the strong evidence that had pointed to Mafia links. "I believe in the justice of the afterlife, not just on earth, and that gives me lots of serenity." A journalist further attenuated the issue of guilt. "If he has been one of the heads of the Mafia, then the Mafia has governed Italy for the last 40 years. My compliments to the Mafia, for how well it has governed." Another expressed an admiring, widely held belief. "He's so smart he never gets caught."

When I hear these cynical attitudes articulated, I find myself suffering, as did my father, who insisted on honesty in civic matters. I think back to Wisconsin and revisit his gloomy presence, locked in his study for a week of late evenings before the April tax deadline. "I could buy several cars," he would lament, "with what I give the government. But hiding money in offshore accounts, that's not what people who love this country do."

2

Forgiveness is a fault line running through Italian society. Like a fault line, its tremors, as well as its invisible presence, are useful to remember. Some scenes, like Pope John Paul II meeting with his accused assassin, Ali Ağca, in prison and accepting his admission of remorse ("I have spoken to him like a brother and I have pardoned him and he has my complete trust"), ultimately have political repercussions. (The meeting supported his eventual early release and transfer to a Turkish jail.) The scene, which was elaborated on in Italian talk shows and public debates, represents nearly two thousand years of a story that draws respect from all citizens in Italy regardless of their politics. Compassion, an idea to be reproposed publicly, sometimes in secular language, sometimes in religious words, surfaces in many forms and accompanies even economic decisions. Even if it is a more superficial emotion, the admission that judging is always difficult, that criminals, too, have families, seems to coexist within public opinion asking for justice. The perception that guilt may not be a sufficient reason for punishment is one that affects some outcomes; I am not alone here in struggling with its negative consequences for public trust.

3

Forgiveness has many names; the most common falls short of canceling the offense: It becomes tolerance. In Italian terms, it is considered as normal as eating. It can be overdone. But just as traffic circles depend on making decisions—using basic rules about when to enter—tolerance, if not forgiveness, heavily and nervously persists as part of the process of handling relationships in a society

where mobility is limited and conflicts and injustices drag on for decades. Forgiveness and how it works has the pragmatic spin that it shares with the zip of the traffic circle. One enters and plays, even though infractions are occurring right and left. Over and over, the offender has vanished by the time one exits. The debate occurs by honking madly or making rude gestures.

4

Thirty years after the terrorist act in which eighty-eight people died when a bomb exploded in the Bologna train station, the tragedy has not been solved. On each anniversary, the national news debates the crime, the failure of the judicial system to uncover the truth, and each year the survivors' cries for resolution deepen so that with closure, forgiveness can take place. This incident is one in a long string of terrorist events that are still clouded and tangled in political knots, Cold War secrets, Vatican secrets, Mafia secrets inside of which citizens assume there is an answer that could be known if there were political will. The shadows that persist, starting from the undeclared civil war in the north of Italy at the end of World War II, make many attempts at justice dark exercises. Resisting the reconciliation commissions that European countries like Germany and Spain established, Italy to this day has not been successful in opening up these years for transparent inspection.

5

The element of tolerance in Italy is the single most compelling element that catches me off guard. Some metaphorical aspect of the *condono*, as well as of forgiveness, deeply appeals. Acknowledging this makes me recognize the young girl who always pestered her parents, hoping to find broader, less literal views. It surprises me how frequently economic costs or even assigning guilt are not the first lines of debate in Italy when evaluating a problem in which a decision about life needs to be taken. A minor example would be the Humane Society in Parma, which boards dogs as long as they live, once their owners abandon them. The reasoning is: Why should animals be put down when they have done nothing wrong?

Outlawing the death penalty is a far more powerful example. Italy's opposition to it is a basic pillar of its modern society. It arises from earlier models of progress, nestled as far back as the gladiators and the transformation of Roman society by eliminating cruel sport and punishment. The Italian constitution, written after the horrors of World War II, forbids capital punishment. It ended a practice reintroduced by Mussolini. Since the initial statute prohibiting civil courts from applying capital punishment, its use also has been eliminated from military ones.

Italy's constitution, ratified in 1947, is considered one of the best in the world. Forged with an idea of a collectivity, bringing together in a single democracy parties and groups that had not only recently been enemies but also historically were not in simple agreement, it provided for plurality. The common ground was equality for all, and these collective definitions brought about conditions for compromise as progress.

The prolonged and obvious crisis in Italian government in recent years, which seems unfathomable to citizens of some Western democracies, rightly can be considered as a degenerate form of tolerance. The infractions of public interest or decency represent that attitude in its worst forms: indifference, denial, or pseudorealism (that is, we have no other solution to offer).

But tolerance does not lead Italians to tolerate the intolerable when at last it mortally offends them and they realize its dangers. Then they will apply reason and discipline, and join forces to restore tolerance to a place of dignity. The recent toppling of the prime minister under the pressure of an imminent financial crisis and the solution of replacing him with a "technical government" headed by a nonelected prime minister and nonelected cabinet secretaries express exactly that abrupt reaction after seemingly interminable acceptance. Voters ultimately didn't make the decision, nor did members of Parliament. But all concurred that it had to be done. The president of the republic found a way to make it happen. Political parties that had been locked in opposition agreed to obey this man with honorable credentials. The intractable prime minister obeyed and stepped down. The existence of the technical government is another form of a *condono*. This time, the grace period has been designed for the political parties that were unable to carry out reforms.

XI

Centuries After

To you your rights, to me mine.

—a motto written by Giovanna da Piacenza, 1524

1

In 2008, the city of Parma held a celebration for the nine hundredth year of its cathedral. The large square blocks of strong, beautiful sandstone had been polished and cleaned until the varied tones in the façade looked as if they were illuminated by permanent moonlight. As a part of the commemoration, elaborate scaffolding, which was in place for more than six months, took 300,000 visitors within a few feet of the domes of San Giovanni Evangelista and Santa Maria Assunta, both of which had been frescoed by Correggio over a period of ten years, starting in 1520.

I made four trips to the top in those months, accompanying visiting friends. Gradually, I became conscious of the painter's accomplishment. To stand that close to his work in the Duomo was to be bathed in a vision that all but put a woman on a par with Christ. She, too, was without sin; she, too, was physically assumed into heaven after death, according to Catholic doctrine. Largely sustained by folk tradition, the special facts of her life without sin grew larger and larger, even though in the fourth century, the Godhead had been defined without her. She grew anyway and her feast days were central to the life of cities, towns, and villages. "Mary, loving mother, Mary, loving, Mary, loving, Mary, loving mother."

We on the platform were included in the dizzying celestial winds where the entire lot of biblical humanity was waiting for her elevation. The colors—warm persimmons, yellow ochers, pinks, and willow greens—the bare feet of foreshortened evangelists: The dense experience captured a new chapter of humanity being lifted toward equality. Mary's open arms embraced that opportunity.

Correggio, while freeing the body—freeing women and thus men—also introduced another radical vision. He used human bodies to define the perspective, creating a sense of infinity. The sky, without any architectural features to frame it, became a far simpler and less mediated illusion. Human beings—historical figures and human forms—established the perimeters of the beyond. In this way, human beings were the center of a universe that was shown then as unlimited sky. His was a first picturing of a new relationship to the heavens. The fresco presented the image that without buildings, without institutions, cornices, things, humans and their history were in a far more immediate relationship to the universe. Correggio's solution telescoped what would soon be confirmed by Copernicus, Galileo, and Bruno. Humanity existed in history and was positioned in a universe that was not confined by a Church that saw the Earth as fixed.

In the locked-down frost of dark January, I planned to stand in line for the last time—the last time probably in my lifetime was the exact thought—and was bereft to discover that the exhibition had finally closed, leaving no more chances for an extraordinary examination of what could only be called "a vision." In the four visits in which I and others trudged up the hundred metal stairs, with feet thudding as if we were a buffalo herd, alchemy had taken place, particularly in the cathedral, where three hundred feet above the altar, Mary, the mother of Jesus, was waiting to ascend into an infinite heaven.

2

The curve of the dome circled the hundred of us standing on the metal platform, as if skimming our heads with a huge wing. The

windows, the cornices, all the physical details of the brick structure suddenly made the dome into a room. The figures, which
for years I had struggled to make out, since from the ground level
of the cathedral they are minute, are larger than life-size bodies.
Having been designed using the rules of foreshortening, up close
they are oddly deformed, as they assume forms that adjust for the
curved shape.

Mary, seen through binoculars, had never seemed particularly expressive. Up close, she was nearly bursting, as if she had
trained to withstand the immense energies that would assault her
as she ascended. The ecstatic woman, standing among the important figures of Old and New Testament history, was about to do
what only one other figure in history had done. An atmosphere
like light rippled and swayed through the painted crowd. Slightly
off center, Mary was in the process of assuming the primary focus,
once she was reached by the descending figure buffeted by winds.

3

In that decade between 1520 and 1530, when Correggio painted a message of movement and liberation, women were both within reach of and in danger of losing their place in public society. The bodies as well as the minds of women were coming out of hiding, expressing independence and passion. Correggio was able to map this out, until the local priests saw the pink thrashing flesh as writhing snakes, and the Church in Rome, pressed by many political threats, condemned such notions.

They had already shut down the room in Parma in which Correggio had painted *Diana* as part of a series of playful and enigmatic scenes. Giovanna da Piacenza, the abbess of the Convent of San Paolo, who commissioned the painter to decorate her ceiling, was forced to stand by as her Benedictine order was cloistered in 1524, after losing a power struggle in which she challenged three Popes to continue the women's enlightened and self-interested independence, which had been decreed four centuries earlier.

For four centuries, twenty-four noblewomen had run the convent autonomously and had carried on managing family land, mills, banking, diplomacy, and supporting the arts. The secular scene Correggio had depicted in Giovanna's room, without reference to a Christian God, without coherent theology, and including magical pagan references to fate and destiny, needed to disappear from view, as did a general climate of disorder; thus the Church cloistered the women. Correggio's choice to paint the abbess on the central fireplace as the huntress Diana, with her finger pointing directly at the rear end of a horse with a lifted tail, a horse that popular interpretation claimed was a representation of the Pope, could not have aided her case.

Once Correggio was working women toward a central and independent place, and the human body in the cathedral's central space served as a way of framing heaven, a radical message spread out across the ceiling of the cathedral. Depicting Mary was not the most controversial element. She was almost an incidental victim of a climate of insecurity brought about in a Church made vulnerable by the Reformation and pressures from the Holy Roman Empire. It would only be a matter of a few years before, as we would put it today, the dome became politically incorrect because of paranoia that perceived flesh as evil and writhing. The Catholic Church of the Counter-Reformation, pressured by the existence of Protestants and new models for the universe that disputed church doctrine, reined in its members by using censorship and punishment.

Correggio left Parma in 1530, satisfied with his massive, radiant composition. But he was troubled by judgment of his work as lascivious and difficult to grasp. The difference between what the local priests saw as real and what he saw made it a tragedy to insist that they were looking at the same dome.

Death swiftly followed. Dispirited, he died at age forty-four. Giovanna da Piacenza also died, her heart broken, six months after she had lost her freedom and was cloistered in 1524. Terror lies

in those two deaths caused, in some way, by the effects of a political upheaval. But there are more ramifications. They are the subtle and pervasive ones arising from a general climate of repression
and fear that works so well ordinary people shrink to conform to
ideological distortions until they are unable to perceive themselves as confused, blind, or frightened. They accept what authority tells them. In matters of art as well as social policy, in that state,
then and now, most of us can be banally herded into believing a
mass deception.

4

I like to imagine that Giovanna and Correggio knew that there
would be other centuries, other times for interpreting their discoveries and lives. Whether or not that is true or if it comforted them,
who can say? Invisibly present in their choices to express radical
ideas was a prevailing view of time: a future that always made reference to the past. Did they make some of their choices based on
that perception: the long view, the importance of challenging
what they knew was false? Would this conviction of vindication in
a time that they would never live to see have been consolation if
you were cloistered, as Giovanna was? Would it have been worth
more than gold ducats, if you were Correggio, who missed basking
in fame? Is this view something to bite into, not as sweet as success, but still tasting of hope because it offers an explanation for
why knowledge survives ignorance? These questions touch anyone
writing or living now.

XII

Rosina

Io, they have been so bad to me this morning.

—Rosina at her window

1

From the moment I had enough money to rent my apartment in the courtyard, Rosina was a de facto focus. Then and now, she remains an interlocutor, a presence that is reincarnated in every immigrant who stands on a corner with an open hand. Rosina, because of the social fabric, never begged. She had the stability of place and a community. She always looked out from her window, like a large sunflower facing the cavelike entrance to the courtyard and turning her head with its progressing events. Starkly framed by her solitary condition, she lived, in part, on the novelties that unfolded when someone walked through the passage. She intruded in conversations and leaned on the relationships to help her. "Io," she would cry out with a tremulous voice that rose. "Io, they have been so bad to me this morning."

Rosina was a remarkable human being, whom I remember for her patience with a life that was pain-filled. When I lived in the yard, I thought of her existence as absurd. I linked her boredom and passivity to Beckett and to essays by Camus, specifically Camus's autobiographical work about his inarticulate, half-mute mother. The tension for me was always that Rosina was not a character in someone's work, but a person whom I saw every day.

Camus located an inarticulate reciprocal love that both he and his mother shared. Camus's mother became a presence as vast as the sea, as much a part of him as the sky. I came to see Rosina's essence, her ability to sustain her incredibly difficult life, as beyond my capacity to interpret. I came to see her as a person brave enough to live a life that had few obvious satisfactions and no familial love. She survived because of a collective response and her inclusion in the ongoing life of the courtyard. She also faced life by using her own resources, often a kind of hypnotic prayer. Rosina is an eternal question, without an answer, but not really, if answers can be scaled to compassion and community. Rosina was kept alive by social relationships with others, others who also had very little but who believed in human need.

Rosina was not a saint, nor were any of us. Sometimes all of the women hanging out of their windows would shout at her, telling her to shut up, or would criticize her for her prayers. The mood in the yard would flutter briefly, as if a group of pigeons was being disturbed. But at the end of the day, voices always cried out to her, gave a sympathetic word or two, offered her medicines that might be dropped in a basket on a string and then relayed by another neighbor to her window. She was dosed with many things that probably were not good for her, but she took the advice and tried the salve.

Rosina is an eternal question about suffering and poverty that cannot be measured by any statistic. She is the person who is nearly helpless, the person who does not want charity, who may never be productive. She was alive, and her moans, her crying out, made her a conscience in the courtyard. She was a daily rasp wearing down denial of the sort that lets beggars be denied. She cried out with need, at the same time that she showed she was doing everything within her power to do her best. She kept people human and forced them outside of clichés and abstractions about poverty. If Rosina was in trouble, we as members of the courtyard were also in trouble. She was part of us.

2

Rosina leaned out, always at the window, because she was alone, in pain, and poor. She didn't work, because she could not and because

a pittance called charity paid for her small claims on existence. Sitting, she could watch and be part of the drama of fights and the lives
of the cats, the furniture makers, and the market people. She wanted
to do good for others, those who talked to her from high and low
windows. Her solution was to pray. Sometimes it got on people's
nerves. Her shaky voice, and her sorrow—and, when the furniture
makers were cruel to her, playing on her vulnerability, making dirty
jokes about her underwear hanging on the string line, leaving a
cockscomb, a male symbol, on her sill, her cries about injustice and
her slow, unrelenting repositioning of herself through her prayers—
circled every corner of the yard, and sometimes shutters banged
closed in protest. Rosina could be baited so easily that the furniture
makers never tired of hearing her wounded shrieks. Her cat, Moro,
swollen or fat from all the lungs she fed him, was also tortured by
them. That would make her scream at the top of her voice. But she
continued to hold to her rosary and its way of directing her mind.

As alone as she was, Rosina's presence was dignified. While
she remained close to the edge, she never slipped off into depres-
sion. Her gray hair was clean, straight; her cotton dresses or her
heavy sweater were nondescript, faded, and devoid of any brightness or smartness, but washed. She embodied the question most
Italians ask themselves: How can we sleep or have care from a
doctor if we know that others cannot have it? How can we eat if
someone else is without bread?

She had a horribly twisted spine. Once a week, after moaning
in pain to get down the step near her door, she dragged herself to
go out to the shops. She would get lung for the cats and perhaps
chicken livers for herself. The butcher whom she used was less
than five feet tall. He stood on a high platform and could cut meat
as transparently thin as handkerchiefs. His skill is of a time that is
gone and perhaps forgotten. He could get eight slices for scaloppine
out of a quarter pound of veal when I had guests. Stropping a knife
that was as long as his arm, he wielded the sharpened blade to reach
even greater heights of precision; he cut the meat like gold leaf.

3

Up and down the Via del Pellegrino, the skills of poverty, of saving, skills of needing less, hummed in the way shopping bags were never full, the way empty crates were whisked from the streets. There was a language of dignity fished from what had been discarded by others. The sauces made from two ripe tomatoes and a leaf of basil or the tight, straight net of woolen threads that could close large holes in sweaters to keep them circulating—the skills of poverty were highly polished in the courtyard, even though it seemed close to the bottom of Rome's social scale. Even in the smelly courtyard, there was a sense of order. People did sweep. In the bare apartments, floors were washed and smelled of pine Lysol. Food was well arranged. Continuity and tradition went on like altars that offered security and places to light candles.

Rosina was not knowable in most ways, but she was solidly formed by religious beliefs and her care for her black cat, Moro. Her routine built up into a presence that was understood, in part, by seeing her and not looking away. It became quite natural to sit with Rosina in the room that was as damp as if water was running down the walls. In spite of the way I hoarded time for my writing, passing her lonely and cheerful face before I climbed my stairs, I often gave in. The plot could wait. We would eat what I took from my cupboard.

Rosina had no plans, no bourgeois schemes for promotion or change. Time passed through her, and its naked emptiness never overtook her fully, dragging her all the way down.

4

The Etruscan she-wolf is aggressive and fierce. She is wild and knows a world that can be intuited and followed by instinct. The she-wolf belongs to poetry. She evolved as generative, original, a

very ancient embodiment of sacredness. Not Rosina, not practical boss Minica, the she-wolf draws power from intricate intelligence, using her senses and her keenly loyal nature. She faces the unknown directly. Looking into the dark, she scrutinizes it, on guard. She knows what belongs to her. Capable of nurturing, even creatures foreign to her species, her care generated civilization itself. The mystery in that mythical act has been told for more than two thousand years.

Why that conclusion should come up now, I don't know. But there it is, a pagan image of animistic, sacred, and undefeatable power, insisting to be placed alongside a description of Rosina, perhaps because the question of suffering and our interest in denying it as a communal problem is so strong. Or, perhaps, it came to mind because the she-wolf's instincts, which brought civilization to the world, involved nurturing life, even when the creatures demanding to be fed were not her own.

XIII

Newspapers

I won't change jobs—I promise—and I'll go on writing what happened and what I think.

> —Maurizio Belpietro, editor of *Libero*, after an
> assassination attempt, 2010

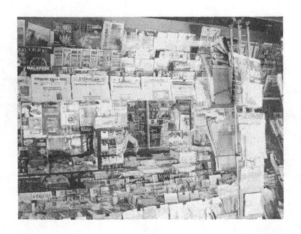

1

Over morning coffee, before I start my writing, I skim an article on the Italian philosophers Croce and Gentile. They are called *esterofili*, those influenced by outside, or foreign, thinkers. This can be seen in their serious lapses in analyzing idealism. From there I pick from the same article thoughts supported by references to earlier philosophers:

Everything that can be said about content leads to original discoveries.

This is important because it testifies to what language calls truth.

Heraclitus wrote that error confirms the existence of truth, because without error, there would be no truth.

Error con-firms; that is, holds firm, makes solid the truth—truth that "has a heart that does not tremble."

This intense presentation of evidence is absorbed before eight o'clock from the *Corriere della Sera*. Italy has always cheered me up with its hearty doses of heavy cultural reading found in the daily newspaper. It's an "of course," without that shallow, destructive tautology that whispers, It won't sell; people won't read it. They will read it because fingering the past makes the pressure of the present bank crises, Mafia arrests, the fading fortunes of Milan's soccer team assume less stressful proportions. And the cost of newsprint, by law, is subsidized by the government.

At the newsstand, the papers of all political persuasions are hung, one next to another, so that the headlines often bang like dissonant bells. Like a neighbor's laundry, they can be read openly for comparisons, and thus expose language as a tool for promoting bias, while providing evidence for being skeptical about truth. The stand, ingeniously crammed with magazines with fancy covers—cars, nude women, men with bulging muscles, lavish pasta dishes, woeful saints, blindingly shiny kitchens and sleek bedrooms, photos of miracles and shrines—always offers counterbalancing, sober book series to collect, often sponsored by the newspapers themselves. At the moment, classics written by social thinkers, including Rousseau, Darwin, and Gandhi, are being sold twice a week, for one euro each, plus the cost of a paper. They are accompanied by introductions that explain their significance and context. Voltaire's *Treatise on Tolerance* ("I detest your opinion but I will defend until death your right to express it") is next.

Stopping at the newsstand is a daily ritual as popular as getting a coffee. The habit is generally of a more cultural nature than what takes place in bars and tobacco shops, which enable, in a moderately respectable way, gambling, smoking, and two or three

drinks before going to work. Children frequent newsstands on weekends for their favorite trading cards and comic books. And amid all the common attractions, the act of making culture available is a regular, planned event. Here, for pittances and a participant's willingness to keep up with series that extend for as long as thirty weeks, books can be had on history, art, literature, musicians, centuries of furniture, regional and foreign cuisine, stamps. These collections are authoritative texts that put culture within reach, removing its association with privilege. When the corner newspaper stand closes for vacation, it can wreak havoc with a season's careful accumulation of the treasures of ancient Greece or Rossini's librettos and accompanying CDs. Volumes twenty-six, twenty-seven, and twenty-eight may have to be begged from a stand open in another part of town, where they have been promised to someone else. For the next three weeks, a series on contemporary authors is featuring Oriana Fallaci's books. The first, *Letter to an Unborn Child*, is her autobiographical essay on the meaning of her abortion.

XIV

Parallel Lives

I don't know if I could marry someone from another *contrada*.

—young dentist in Siena

1

Until I lived in Siena for about a month, I never realized how much distance there was between Florence and Siena. There is much to be discovered about identity by trying to sketch out the differences between two cities that are less than one hour from each other and whose governments were in direct conflict nearly seven hundred years ago. I hope to show what may not be completely evident: Each city in Italy has its own way of coping with its long history.

I lived in Siena, instead of visiting it as a tourist, in the late 2000s when I was asked to teach writing to a group of American students. Many discoveries came from weeks in the students' residence, in which I had a small garretlike space, overlooking the city's ubiquitous red roofs. The time to myself, tucked away in a room with windows that started from the floor, gave me a sense of responsibility only to myself, to enjoy the solitude, light, and freedom of being alone in a room with a simple desk with red metal legs and an even simpler unpainted bed.

Suspended from commitments of daily life in Parma, I could focus intensely on my students, but then I still had the better part of the day to feel time as elastic and attractive energy. The silence in the room and a sensation of choices that fell to me without any particular call to duty, however, swelled into growing uneasiness. I had a sensation that I was slightly lost. Perhaps it issued from the perception that too much was unaddressed and building up in my life. Or maybe it was simpler. I was feeling the tensions of balancing two identities that tottered when I had to explain one culture to another.

2

Teaching students from America was new territory for me. The gap in our ages was a chasm that I perhaps had never experienced as sharply with the students I normally teach in Italy. For them, a word like *bourgeois* was out of the Dark Ages. Once a defining category, it was anathema to these young faces whose eyes were puffy with sleep as they dragged themselves up the hill and entered a classroom next to the church where Manzoni's youngest daughter, Matilde, was buried.

In Parma, where I had first met them for a two-day introduction, I had tried to construct a timeline of human habitation, starting with gray chipped obsidian Paleolithic tools found in soil around the city's hills and on display in the archaeological museum. As we stood near a Neolithic grave in the museum's basement, where bones of two bodies formed circles, the guide spoke of birth and death as a circle. Some yawned and some sat down. When the guide asked about what significant discovery was made in the Neolithic that led to the reorganization of human society, we entered an embarrassed silence. "Was it food?" a thoughtful young woman asked, opening the way.

Further on, we stopped in front of a Roman tombstone that had been paid for by a Roman slave who purchased his freedom and left his story—his name, his freeing of himself, his profession as a dyer of cloth, his wish to perpetuate his name and the name of his family—all carved in a piece of marble about three feet high. I tried to impress on them the importance of writing, then. The importance of words. How the Roman slave lived on two thousand years after his death because he had recorded the facts of his life and its transitions. Many of the students were sending text messages by now, beholden to a sense of the present that was conversational and not linked to place.

It was easy enough to remember my young self in Rome and to stop my mind from making comparisons between Italian students and American students or more general judgments about their knowledge. Youth can change in any direction overnight. I was only curious to understand how they conceived of their lives and to try, even failing if I had to, to bring them to a level where time opened new horizons. Then, having so much space for myself, I wanted to learn about the city and to discover where I was, too, in the trajectory of a hot summer that had followed many difficult years.

3

I didn't know how to evaluate the students' lack of awareness. As surprising as it might have seemed that they did not acknowledge their debt to the Neolithic, it was more relevant that many of them did not really know what a verb was, nor did they follow the news, or have basic literary or philosophical references. Rightly or wrongly, I took this as a sign of the neglectful acceptance of a society where basically bright, decent kids had to take on two jobs just to pay for an education that no longer required the systematic study of world history, literature, and science. The students were agreeable and easy. Many professed their subject of study to be communication. Several came armed with official documents of learning disabilities. They felt like cultural orphans to me, needing, among other things, to meet a seasoned adult who believed that the idea of studying history was not an elective one.

4

Siena, with its high walls and hilly streets, steep and unalterable over centuries, is a place nearly stopped in time. The guidebook I procured proclaims it, in a somewhat understated observation, a city "which has succeeded in keeping its original medieval appearance intact over the years." Nothing in the central area can be expanded, and cars and buses, heavily restricted, can barely pass between the walls at many points. The geography of the city and its preservation of the medieval palaces and towers, as well as the low redbrick apartment buildings, fix its identity, starting from the sublime space of the Piazza del Campo.

Here offered up is the unusual, wide, nine-sectioned Campo, which is so inclusive and organically rounded that it seems a sea creature—like a medusa without the tentacles, a creature that breathes quietly in and out. The beauty of the inclined shell that slopes toward the Palazzo Pubblico turns the Piazza del Campo, with its rich, dizzying herringbone pattern, into a space unlike any other in the world. Surrounded by the municipal architecture curving around it, the whole oval is a kind of psychoanalytic picture of identity.

The Piazza del Campo is more than the heart of the city. It is a dream that suggests a dream. It is man-made. There is no nature, none of the countryside outside of the walls where cypress rise like dark green smoke and bleached golden fields contrast with the mountains of stone. The piazza, with its imaginary bivalve, the Gaia Fountain, which bears the name of the earth goddess, with Mary in bas relief at the center of its white rectangular sides, and Adam and Eve being driven out of Eden, offers such sublimity, such elegance, that crossing it makes almost anything afterward seem lacking in imagination, even crass. The beauty, useless, extravagantly sublime—all the herringbone bricks so obviously handmade and hand-laid—exists just to make us marvel. The Campo's slope, the way it reaches all around like an open palm, an offering that is being made without begging for something in return, defines each and every person crossing it as a possessor of an unimaginable wealth that any other human being also can inherit.

The Gaia Fountain to one side flows generously and suggests an antique Roman pool where people might sit around. The little

black mutts with curls in their tails, the fathers pushing strollers, the old women crossing the bricks, the junk shops and souvenir shops with their *contrada* flags and their vinegar cruets, their key chains made in China, their linen dish towels with lemon prints—all these fit around the edges and add life.

The American students, too, walked in the shell, walked across it, came to know the streets feeding out and into it by name, and they felt amazed. There is no other word for how they felt. They did not know such a shell existed and that they would feel a part of its mysterious curves. They learned how to buy chunks of *pan-forte*, with its ginger and cinnamon, but they also learned to refer to the Campo not in terms of time, its seven hundred years, so much as in terms of beauty. They came to see its beauty as a dimension that they had not come across before. One young woman student proposed that the university offer scholarships so that more students could visit Italy and see for themselves another way of life. With the exception of two, they were nearly indignant that such a world had been unknown to them before they left what was before their eyes at home.

They had lived so close to the present—its shopping centers, its freeways, its playing fields—that in some profound way they were surprised by what they could enter and be a part of in Siena, even though they saw it as slow and often inefficient. Their homes were probably not poor, and probably were no different from many others in America, but they were dull homes, where much of the focus of education emphasized getting future jobs. There seemed to be little time in these families for translating skill into pleasure with no immediate use. There seemed to be little curiosity in such families for how things could be different: for instance, cooking with two tomatoes and a basil leaf and sharing it, or playing games where no one lost. In Siena, for these kids in their first weeks, there was cheap wine and food that didn't come out of a package or microwave. Then beauty began to raise questions.

5

To walk across the Piazza del Campo in early morning, when sunlight has appeared with the street sweepers and with the barmen who are washing down awnings and dusting the chairs that will be set out and soon filled by tourists, was a pleasure I could not deny myself each day that I was there. Pigeons were often bathing

in the fountains. I bought an early paper and then refused to open it, feeling as if the news would impinge on the near innocence that I felt by entering that space. Although I did usually catch two or three blasts coming from eighteen-point headlines, I resisted getting worked up over proclaimed corruption. Cigarette smokers, three-wheeled garbage trucks, pigeons, now washed, and occasionally turning in angled curves so that their wings whirred gold and their stolid natures were obliterated for a second or two, worked against the overriding sensation of being nearly alone. The possessiveness one feels being nearly alone in such a place makes one feel overly important, special, and then comes a wave of panic that one will appear a pretender. For beauty does raise questions of how much, how recent, how false, and how escapist it is, if set against a backdrop of real life. Yet the fact that it is collective and cannot be bought or sold, but only shared, eliminates inklings of guilt.

6

In the Piazza del Campo, there is no time outside of the Middle Ages, and thus a feeling of fixed forms and pristine consistency is palpable. In Siena, the walls around the city, the gates, and the towers are all of the same brick, a red called Siena red. There is one significant edifice for government, the municipal palace, and one for religion, the cathedral, Santa Maria Assunta; both contribute to a feeling that the city is a model, an ideal, with unalterable roots. The fixed patterns of the city are not mummifying ones, but they create a sense of a base back in time. I don't know if this adds to a feeling of dream, but the physically clear sense of identity in ancient buildings and in works generated by the school of Sienese painters who lived centuries ago made something happen that I never would have grasped had I not lived in my little attic room and had time to think without resorting to conversations.

If I had not taught for a month, and thus had the chance to see the city and understand it enough to make students explore it for what it is or might be, I would still basically be putting forth an idea of Siena, a city mediated by movements, painters, and architecture. More personal perceptions emerged from the month spent—in fact, three.

First, I came to discover the *contradas*, physical neighborhoods founded at least three centuries ago that broke the city up into seventeen local divisions. The life inside of these groups today is vivid and allowed me to experience the intense, partially imaginary or, better, symbolic life that accompanies living in a walled city that offers a fixed, dreamlike model for the ideal. Second, I came to sit in front of Duccio's Madonna until I could rest there without a sense of time. This turned into a meditation. Third, I came to understand more deeply the differences between Florence and Siena. During this time, I felt how being born a citizen of Siena or of Florence made your sense of self differ, starting from the early days of your birth. In Siena, you would be given a ceremonial baptism in a *contrada*, which defined you for the rest of your life, while in Florence, you would absorb an image of centuries of masculine genius that connected you to the world.

7

The Palio di Siena is a series of horse races abhorred by animal rights advocates, and known around the world primarily because of the most important contest, which occurs in August on the date that commemorates Mary's assumption into heaven. The race, which lasts for approximately two minutes, is a complete dash by jockeys riding bareback on horses around the shell-shaped piazza, which has been covered with a clay surface. The horses, goaded into going faster, sometimes skid into barriers, or slip on the curves, and break legs. They are shot, if they are irrecoverably injured, soon after the few minutes of glory. Most, however, finish, prancing, ready to go again. Some who sustain injuries are kept alive by a collective pension fund for horses that have run the race.

Who, then, could imagine that, just as the Etruscans, who devoted themselves to building underground tunnel systems for games and tricks, the Sienese, in these two minutes, express a set of preparations and actions that hold more emotion than even a soccer team's fortunes? The analogy to the Etruscans is not that far off, since competition in the city is a yearlong focus, not simply symbolic but also an orchestrated set of clever moves, strategizing, and secrets, where each *contrada* has an ally and an enemy. Each has a bank, a church, a meeting place, a country club–like residence, and each has sets of rules that must be honored and sets of rules that can be broken. In the long months of preparation for the race, time periods are set aside for ritual displays of masculinity, in which beating up your enemy is allowed, bad language is tolerated, and elaborate pranks are encouraged. Church rules are bent in certain circumstances. Indeed, the local church that belongs to each *contrada* allows its horse to be led to its altar before the race. The horse is blessed, and the rider is blessed, and the strange mixture of sacred and profane, that safety valve built into a life of regulated appearances—the rumpus aspect of life, the days of Carnival before Lent, the absolving confession, the incredible rituals and transgressions that make conforming to appearances or rules or unchanging arrangements tolerable because of a tacit agreement to a parallel life where other rules and other exceptions prevail—appears as the principle that governs *contrada* members.

8

The students' perception of *contrada* life was understandably different from mine. Without the language, without the history, how could they interpret it as anything but marvelously inclusive? Since one of the students was making a documentary on a *contrada*, the students as a group visited a specific one night after night and began to be recognized and feel included on the gorgeous terrazzo, where tables were laid out for meals, where films or music were being offered on the lawn overlooking the city, where cards were being dealt at other tables, where food was subsidized and members of the *contrada* served and cleaned up tables while children romped through the whole area and older people picked them up if they tumbled or sent them back to parents if they were lost. Above was usually a starry indigo sky; just below it, the skyline of a few of the most prominent churches and the orange halogen streetlights set up patterns; and all around the terrace on the hills, inky cypresses were whirling their branches or nodding, depending on the breeze.

The students were welcome to stay, welcome to slip in even at midnight for a cheap glass of wine, or welcome to sit with the English-speaking fellow who was a *contrada* member, flattered to talk about *contrada* life. There was never an issue of not belonging or buying a membership for all the services offered to them.

The students didn't seem to see the evenings as tinged with irony. Although the young man explained that he was a dentist with no real chance for full-time work, although he spoke Italian and English and spoke both equally well, they were unable to imagine the way the *contrada* activity compensated for an angst that bubbled up from time to time. The *contrada* was a lifetime identity, conferred at birth, defined in part by neighborhood, or class. It was something the dentist considered an obstacle for marriage, should he be forced to choose between a spouse's *contrada* or his own. Only one *contrada* thus far allowed women to lead it, to head the council with its forty voting members. And one of the key elements was making people feel they belonged, so that often the council was composed largely of elders. They were often conservative, but they needed, according to the dutiful dentist, to be listened to.

The members of the *contrada* composed one big family. One

worked inside the *contrada* as a volunteer, but it was also an obligation; cleaning up the kitchen, cooking for the group, organizing events and publicizing them—all this was part of the ethic. Each *contrada* was an "us." And all but one of the seventeen had a symbolic enemy, "them." And while they no longer fought duels or stabbed one another, each *contrada* had a business manager who, with his advisers, oversaw the financial health of the *contrada*, managed its real estate holdings, and also thought of tricks, false moves, ways of taking the enemy *contrada* into false alliances, particularly in relation to the primary orchestration of the year, the horse race.

9

The young dentist who took us under his wing, hoping that the documentary would help Siena gain respect in the world, invited us into his clubhouse, an imposing modern structure on two floors, with meeting rooms that held cases for the *contrada*'s trophies, going back for centuries. There were jockeys' helmets of metal bashed hundreds of years ago. There were the parchments over centuries declaring a victory in a certain year, each with a design of Mary ascending or in suspension, looking out at her subjects. In still another museum belonging to the *contrada*, this one a deconsecrated church, there were more costumes, and even the coarse, thick tail of a beloved winner, appended to a drawing of the rest of him.

Each *contrada*—Duck, Turtle, Wave, Snail, Ram, and so on—had similar holdings to tell its history and house its members. Most of these went back at least to the seventeenth century, when the *contradas*, which sometimes referred to a geographical area in the city and at other times to a military company, began to run regular races with oxen or donkeys, festivities to celebrate visits from rulers or other feast days associated with Mary's life. The holdings are not the rustic lodges or the faux-Gothic temples of groups like the Masons. They are high-profile, elegant meeting places designed by well-known architects who are familiar with the use of glass and beautiful metals like copper. They are competitive, significant expressions of one's group.

As surely as the thread of *contrada* life bound families to their origins, it was also possible to predict that over time, it would be very difficult for an outsider to even wish to belong to something so demanding, since participation and obedience were required in order to obtain the benefits that a group membership would provide. I can think of no analogy to them, not guilds, not university alumni groups, not even church membership. Everything was touched by *contrada* membership, while at the same time, there was a wink to it all, a nod that said it was really a game, really nothing, not real life, and yet as a member, one never had to feel alone, or uncertain of what was next. Gossip was always kept within the group. In theory, one would always have support. In Siena, one had an underground life that was constructed as a race, with a winner, and yet, win or lose, there was always a safety net and a group that made one different from the members of other groups living within the walled city.

10

While the students often stayed past midnight, talking among themselves, I usually went back to my room early. The walk down the first hill and the climb up the next, before reaching the hostel where we were staying, were always magical. There were few people in the streets and the skies were usually clear enough to see the stars. The building facing the hostel had been bombed by the Allies during World War II. With all its blind curves, Siena is a city that is easy to imagine under siege. When I mentioned that the city had been bombed, the students were surprised. One wrote a short story about it and handed it to me. The Americans, as represented by a single GI, fought for three days, and then our protagonist, having defeated those dirty Nazis, went home to JFK Airport as a hero to be greeted by his wife and child.

Reading it, feeling torn about how to explain to him what distressed me about his sincere attempt, I worried, in a way that is never helpful. I foolishly felt despair, as if I could really understand how so many young people were on their own, without dialogue.

11

I have never been one for unnuanced comparisons. Plato's requirement for being a poet, which holds that a touch of madness is essential, is not a condition for those writing prose. In the dentist's ritual world, there is a kind of realism and acceptance of the tyranny of overriding boredom. He is fully aware that the games he adheres to give him a way to exist within a sphere of limited choices.

In our American student's case, he wanted a high-profile job in television. When asked to sit in front of Duccio's *Maestà della Madonna col Bambino e Angeli* and write about silence, he had a panic attack. He couldn't breathe. Weaving his way out of the museum, he got lost, felt choked up, perhaps even because the streets outside had the same meandering and, if you will, suffocating sense of immobility. It may be that he saw more clearly than the other students the closure that was part of living in Siena. And perhaps he also made comparisons and recognized how unprotected he was.

He had to rely on his beleaguered self and forge an identity from a situation of anxiety and lack of financial resources. While he held up his certificate of attention deficit disorder like a shield, he seemed to know, only too well, that it would repel few of life's bullets. He could anticipate a time when military drills would be as far as his support system extended. All I could think to do to help was to go back to his written story. Pointing to the three-day battle, I reminded him that war is long; also, that naming the airport after JFK had not been a thought until, unthinkably, the President had been assassinated.

12

Painting in Siena, the so-called Sienese School, has its first bright period during the time Duccio is working in Florence, Assisi, Siena, and nearby towns. By the time he is painting, sometimes as a student of Cimabue, Siena is the most radical experiment in terms of government on the peninsula. In the period from 1287 to 1355, Siena is governed largely by its middle class, the Council of Nine, which excludes nobles, bishops, feudal lords, or working-class people from holding council positions. It is a period of peace, and the defining structures of the city are erected then. The Palazzo Pubblico, with its high tower and some of the most famous frescoes in Italy on its council walls, is the focal point of the Piazza del Campo. When it was begun in 1290, it emphasized the importance of peace and order and finding ways to include citizens in the business of government. No weapons were allowed in the Campo, no nursing, and no eating of figs. The city, which had known war among its own groups, aimed to quell internecine strife, or at least to raise the level of manners.

The Council of Nine, which was an elected rotating group of citizens who served two-month terms and then retired, was a successful way of opposing or attempting to balance the power of nobles or clans. It worked as a model for over one hundred years. Siena, after it won the Battle of Montaperti against Florence in 1260, never reached a greater height of economic or political power. Perhaps the model of idealization began to be perfected then.

13

The city was one that was devoted to Mary. Mary was a cult figure; in her central role, she harkened back to the Ghibellines, the
landowning faction usually allied with the Holy Roman Emperor
and the non-Church origins of the city. She also arose from the
original founder of the city, the she-wolf who gave birth to both
Rome and, through a mythical grandson, Siena, when the latter
became a Roman colony in the first century B.C.E. Before the 1260
battle with Florence, the townspeople took the keys to the city to
the image of Mary in the cathedral. They laid them at the feet of
"the Queen and Empress of Everlasting Life, the Glorious and
Ever-Virgin Mother of God." She was given credit for the victory
at Montaperti and her cloak was sighted as having laid itself around
the city walls in a gesture of protection. In the most important
two hundred years of Sienese painting, more than half of the
commissions are for Madonnas. Inside the cathedral, each of the
five altars is dedicated to one of Mary's feast days. She becomes
the head of the civic cult in the city.

When Duccio finished his Maestà for the cathedral, in 1311,
bells were rung and trumpets sounded as the enormously complicated two-sided composition was carried through the streets to
the cathedral, where it took the place of the earlier Madonna of
the Large Eyes, which had been worshiped at the time of Siena's
major victory. Bishops and priests accompanied it, as did families,
mostly women and children, who sang and offered prayers.

Timothy Hyman, a British art historian and expert on Siena,
says Duccio's Maestà is "the most irreproducible of all the world's
great paintings; if you lose the scale you lose everything." And
indeed, the central figure of the Madonna is nearly fourteen feet
tall. She has been long removed from the cathedral and now rests
in temperature-controlled semidarkness in the Duomo Museum,
where many of the forty-five panels narrating the Gospel story
originally covering the back of the Maestà remain on two facing

walls. The panels on the reverse side of the *Maestà* were separated from the original composition in the 1700s, when the enormous construction was sawed apart and the front and back were divided forever.

This Madonna, Byzantine in her attitude of contemplation, was the one who caused the panic attack in my student. Probably his reaction was an effect that was almost the opposite of the impact foreseen by the painter. She occupies the center of this huge painting and is redimensioned by a blue mantle larger than she is. Not only does a halo encircle her head with divine energies, but infinity holds her entirely in its blue glove. This midnight blue, Sienese blue, does function differently from the elaborately beautiful gold-and-red embossed mantle that presumably is to be thrown over the blue one. The color suggests a cosmic dimension that makes up part of religious practice. Its symbolism could define a crucial silence that envelops, wraps, surrounds any human life. The blue dominates—something unknowable in large part—because, unlike the other shawl, it is not decorative, not ornamental. It is not a measure or show of worldly treasure. Not dark but deep in hue, the blue mantle holds a space where color transports an energy greater than that of the colors surrounding it. The Madonna is intimately in contact, indeed, covered by the silence of an infinite blue that holds her very life.

14

Before even approaching the other half of Duccio's Maestà, each of the smaller narrative panels, I began to realize that I might never again, after my month in Siena, return to the city. If I did, would it be to visit once more the depth of the Madonna's gaze and the blue embrace of the infinity she participated in? The Maestà was not mine in the way it belonged to anyone from Siena. And while I could associate her sheer size with an enormous and far cruder statue of Minerva I had seen in Rome off and on for all these years, anyone would feel that there was something quite different in how awe was generated and approached in the Roman figure from the way it was in this large image with its mysterious, prescient, and loving expression. Was she a fantasy of a certain period of time, with her golden halo and her Byzantine look of contemplation? How was she conceived? Was she a way of entering another level of meditation; was she divinely inspired?

15

There came a point when I could not bear to think that the day would arrive when I could no longer sit in the air-controlled, darkened room and take in her knowing attitude, the glorious embossed work on the glowing gold halo and cloths surrounding her, and, above all, not see the blue, so deep that it was almost black. Slowly, the painting had entered me: I felt that this blue was working beyond conscious perception, conveying the sensation that there was no knowable end as long as one sat there, guided by the otherworldly gaze of the Madonna.

The *Maestà* expressed an attitude toward reality that was all-encompassing. It belonged to a time when expressing beauty was seen as leading to God, and was a supportive, saving part of everyday life, which also entailed so much hardship and grief. Duccio's painting, in spite of its obvious beauty—the golds, the rhythms—offered up direct knowledge of pain and suffering and included them in a female face, enlarging the experience to sublime acceptance of higher planes of knowledge.

The importance of sublime planes was partially gathered by walking across the Campo. Duccio was able to transport some of this knowledge to his painting, offered as an iconic shrine that could be visited in everyday life. Sponsored by the Council of Nine, and requiring three years of his life to complete, it was meant to provide comfort and a sense of power and glory. It shows a tender framing of grief and the human reality of all that starts at birth and is pondered and held, with the hope that grace will be at work and our unconscious needs will be listened to. His Madonna proposed a story in which any viewer could enter the painting, enter the robe, become the child, and be the child, given the faith expressed in the face of the compassionate mother wearing infinity's cloak.

In contrast, the back side of the *Maestà*, which had been separated three centuries earlier, had been dispersed even further by

selling single panels that now hung in places as far away as Spain
and the United States. Those that remained were stunning not
only for their contrasting colors and brilliant groupings but also for
their clean compositions of the narration of Christ's life and that of
Mary. The fourteen-foot-tall Madonna with Christ, surrounded by
angels and saints, contained a single image that reached back into
earlier histories of Church doctrine and beyond that, to the roots of
humanity's elaboration of maternity. The back of the altarpiece,
which was originally seen not by the congregation but by the priests,
narrated the biblical version of Christ's life and his mother's.

16

I didn't want to leave Siena, in part because of the small room in
which I had lived and come to find hours and hours of silence.
There are always things to be researched: for example, the three
hundred letters of Saint Catherine of Siena, who was interrogated

for heresy but survived and was used as an ambassador for peace, trying to heal the schism between two Popes, one in France, the other in Italy. There were the forty-five sermons of San Bernardino, whose presence in the Campo is marked with a disk to commemorate the time in 1427 when, starting on the day of Mary's assumption into heaven, he conducted a Mass at dawn, followed by a sermon, so that by 7:00 a.m. people were back in the fields or market stalls. His words have been noted down, and his emphasis on honesty, efficiency, responsibility, hard work, and assumption of risk were ethical rules that pertained to the rising merchant class. Iris Origo wrote a beautiful biography of Bernardino, in which she discusses his many homilies that attempted to deepen existing social relationships. "Wrap not up your speech, speak plain and open. Say with your tongue what you hold in your heart."

But research was not my goal. The hours spent in my room, the early hours before I walked the Campo, and the late hours after I had translated for the students at the *contrada*, were ones where I faced an awakening willingness to explore uncertain and broken elements in my own life. I got up looking forward to reentering the city and the fruits of imagination from a period in Siena that was one of relative peace and prosperity. Although the Black Death had taken two-thirds of the population in 1349 and a prolonged famine had decimated the remaining population, intense building and painting had continued to go forward, leaving a legacy of idealized hopes. The entire city, by insisting on maintaining fixed early walls and relying on their messages, challenged death.

17

The murals of *The Blessings of Good Government* and *The Effects of Bad Government*, or *The Well-governed City* and *The Ill-governed City*, by Ambrogio Lorenzetti, painted in the Palazzo Pubblico be-

tween 1337 and 1339, remain an intense interrogation about the process of government and its effects. The proximity and contrast between the two versions make their timelessness an appeal to common sense and rationality. We are above and inside the city in the forty-six-foot panel for peace, where work and life proceed in superimposed seasons and spontaneous angles: Animals are treated kindly, the threshers harvest, the dancers dance, and traders sell their wares, all in close proximity to one another, depicted in a dense, naturalistic, and believably harmonious flow. On the opposite wall, the seriously damaged fresco of *Bad Government*, with its throne of Tyranny and its figures of Cruelty, Deceit, Fraud, Fury, and Greed, shows torture and war, the winter of misery and suffering of all sorts. The allegorical panel on a third wall, uniting the two frescoes, presents a female figure of Justice, who dominates all formulas for creating the conditions for peace. Written nearby: "Love Justice, You Who Judge the Earth."

The students had almost missed this room in the Palazzo Pubblico and a special visit was scheduled for them. Using the intense period of Siena's aspirations for democratic rule, it was not unreasonable to ask the young people to explore their knowledge in order to look for analogies in their country. Few bells went off, but the wall paintings, carrying real examples and dreams from a period of experimentation in government and expansion of business, surprised them. Here in soft tones was a narration about the direct effect of government on lives. The frescoes, painted to last through time, restored several times in various centuries at considerable cost, reached the American students with an impact as powerful as one of Hollywood's efforts. The fact that many stopped and were touched by the fat little pig and the dancers and contrasted the conditions for peace with famine and want meant that Siena's commitment to preserving Lorenzetti's perceptions was worth every lira and euro spent then and now by the city's council members.

These were vivid illustrations, far more complete than photographs of war or famine or torture. The colored plaster visions offered solutions by showing the effect of justice and how providing for all members in society contributed to general prosperity and peace. The loftiness of the proposal—the obvious conclusion—was nearly heartbreaking in its realism. Beauty was man-made in life in Siena, when people were free to live in harmony. The frescos were a fable about local government, in a special moment, overrun neither by foreign powers like Spain, nor by enemy neighbors like the Florentines. The dream of community was a narration including both urban and rural life, both noble and worker, an interrelated system of dependencies and relationships that was in many ways assigned to the population that ruled. The fresco about good government was not a story to make the Sienese feel secure, but to remind them of their own part in their destiny.

The students, even though the afternoon was hot and many wished to sit in cafés, saw, fleetingly, that dark and light vision of government's influence pulled into a third, mediating element: Justice and her sisters. I felt close to the students and their thoughts about the murals. Standing in Italy and talking with the young people about their and my country's role in the world, I felt that past and present, New World and Old, were the same, even though they looked very different on the surface. Government and its elements could be isolated into qualities that either tainted or brightened everyday life. On the walls, we witnessed elementary and powerful truths that needed no elaborate testimony other than the condition of the citizenry. Poverty and suffering could be alleviated or worsened. The balance and which way the scale tipped originated in the definition of justice and the undesirable effects of war.

XV

San Pietrini

Handmade rhythm is powerful and calming.

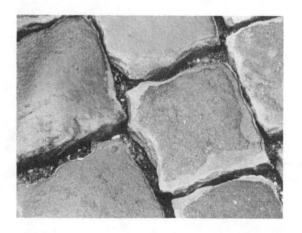

1

I used to carry, in all of my moves, a broken piece of white marble I had found in the courtyard in Rome. Marble exerted a magical effect from the first time I saw its glistening, grainy, and brittle nature up close. In Romanesque works, its salty, unpolished texture had a feeling of dryness, dawn, and shell. As diamonds might for someone else, marble, for me, commanded honor for its beauty and tribute for the horrors and dangers its extrication involved.

Born from metamorphoses, it retains complexity. Formed from dusty limestone heated by volcanic lava and cooled over hundreds of thousands of years, the pink marble from Verona and the white marble from the Apennines of Carrara carry indications of place. Green and violet serpentine marble seduced Roman emperors, who often had it shipped from Africa. Then, since nothing could be set aside, its garish opulence was recycled centuries later, impossible to hide among the more chaste white columns of Italian churches.

Carrara marble was the treasured choice of Italy's greatest sculptors because of its warm whiteness: Its imperceptible blues and grays can be made to suggest nuances of feeling. Polished, it can be made to seem as liquid as water and as soft as a kiss. Its properties are ideal for rendering emotions stirred by flesh. It is far subtler than the Candia marble that is used to make grand edifices sparkle with cool white overstatement.

2

I don't know quite where I lost the marble piece that was one-third of a Roman street sign, but I suspect it was when I had to select the few things that would be shipped to Italy for my permanent move to Parma. Probably I reasoned I would find other pieces of marble. But that was wrong, because this particular one held an important memory. I was prone to giving up too easily what was mine. My piece was part of Rome's system of naming streets, the marble plaques set high in corner buildings. The plaque was deeply and beautifully engraved, with letters that were black at the inside furrows, as was the frame around the rectangle of the sign. Even broken, it looked like an elegant, formal invitation.

I also took a small volcanic black rock with me from Rome, and that survived each of the critical moments my possessions were whittled down before a subsequent move. It still sits in a dish in my living room in Parma, along with seedpods and shells. The volcanic rock is worn on all edges. But once it was probably shaped, flat and squared, polished on top, four squared sides, angled to a convergent point.

The object I'm linking my rock to is called a San Pietrino: a little Saint Peter's stone, a small distinctive shape used to pave the piazza around Saint Peter's Basilica. A real San Pietrino is about the size of a fist, if a fist were square on top and angled underneath. It is a hand-laid stone that composes many of the inner-city streets of Rome and has cousins—as is true of much Roman planning and thinking—in most Italian city centers. The flat patterns it forms are sometimes straight and sometimes fall into half circles. The latter offer a subliminal pulse of progressions, which, if one would take time to study them, would reveal attention to the miracles of mathematical reasoning that made up so much of ancient Rome: the arch and the marvelous gravity-defying dome.

The rock I possess was picked up after a demonstration against the Vietnam War. San Pietrini were natural weapons in emotional battles and they flew when the police gave chase. Roman streets, after an intense demonstration, looked as if they were missing lots of teeth. Tear gas and those paving stones were matched against one another in violent clashes.

The little San Pietrini, which supposedly were conceived for use around St. Peter's in the 1700s, are a result of thinking about what will quickly resolve a practical issue but also last for centuries. Pairing these two qualities is a habit that arises from being wedded to ancient solutions found in the peninsula's riches. In Italy, the use of materials, starting with marble, has always meant taking advantages of basic geological features that then worked their way into the style defining Italian life. Long-lasting, many of the materials are precious ones, obtained by using extraordinary amounts of human labor. Continuity in the access to natural materials assured their continued application. Technologies improved and treatments advanced, but uses of materials that composed interiors and exteriors two thousand years ago have never been replaced or surpassed in floors, staircases, columns, or standards for beauty.

3

My San Pietrino has pattern as its ultimate effect. The paving method is impractical, expensive. At this point, it offers little but a reprimand to mechanical perfection. Able to tease, attract, and calm harried minds, these patterns make cement sidewalks and asphalt roads look mindless. Visual rhythms are difficult to achieve.

Now immigrants bend and make the sound of several iron hammers tapping as piles of stones are pounded into an anchoring layer of sand. Long after you have forgotten about them completely, you see that the pleasant patterns that Marx might have

decried as the result of exploitation—given that human labor is used but not recognized for the specialized skills required—enrich most walks.

The entire press of modern vehicles rolls over them, leaving grease and grime, sometimes loosening the stones from their un-cemented foundations. But their visual delights remain echoes as ancient as the pattern of vines looping from post to post in fields.

The straight laying of San Pietrini stones, a more common arrangement, assumes the sobriety of the early Roman roads. The

Appian Way groans with massive stones dragged into place by slaves. They still function as signs of civilization, awesome, above all, because of the brutal means required to put them in place.

San Pietrini, instead, are light. They go on bearing weight, impervious to local governments pressed to find ways to cut spending. They survive, even in periods of scarce repair, because they are part of urban planning, a language built from the look of cities over centuries, as well as a time-tested practical way of easily repairing a street, without resorting to patches, if there is buckling. They are not startling inventions. Each sturdy stone shaped and laid by hand is part of a simple chant—work.

XVI

Volcanoes and *Terremoti*

And if he sees it coming close, or hears
his well water gurgling agitated,
he frantically collects his wife and children,
and, fleeing with as many of their things
as they can carry, watches from afar . . .
 —Giacomo Leopardi, "Ginestra"
 (translated by Jonathan Galassi)

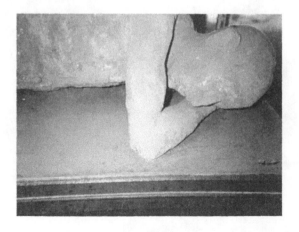

1

Lava as a dried surface is a strong and bewildering material. Lava, regurgitated regularly from Etna, was spewed out in a particularly serious set of explosions in 2002–2003. Fire and ash destroyed nearly forty thousand hectares of the Pineta Ragabo on the north side of Mount Etna, killing two tourists and leaving a stretch of charred emptiness that was sobering. Guided by the Italian forestry rangers, who were sponsoring a conference at which my husband was speaking, the walk on lava was in some ways an afterthought. The rangers' focus was forest trees and human beings' long relationship to the forest. The sudden spill from one of the northern seams had left its hardened black rock over an area that had once been full of trees and eliminated 10 percent of Etna's carefully protected forests. The ashy, hard, grayish black cover molded the hills into a moonscape.

Walking on the choppy lava waves was difficult because of their sharp unevenness. I couldn't find flat surfaces for my feet and fell several times. Black undulations over the landscape, in all directions, a steady blackness that was intransigent, impressed with its far-reaching effects, as natural devastation does. The porous carbonized surface went on as far as the eye could see. All life had been licked up except for weird deviant patches. Charcoal stumps and rare green scrub pushed through here and there. After nearly an hour of walking, we reached a point where the lava came to a stop. There was ash and a wall of burned trees and no life and then there were singed trees and then there was land that was untouched by the molten flow. Part of the landscape had been wiped out and reshaped, and part flourished, green, untouched.

Farther up, where the suffocating material from the volcano's vents had not flown and burned, we were taken through hectares of white Swedish birch. The birch grew in meadows, flowing meadows, and the guide said that the trees had been pushed south over time by the cooling of the climate that caused the last glaciation. The volcano's steep sides were a laboratory of experiments and tricks.

2

Etna is so large that although we walked for the better part of the morning, we stayed on the north side and never managed even a peek at the top cone, which we saw so clearly as a point when we looked out over the horizon from the village of Taormina. But if we had any doubts about the firepower of the volcano, we saw its far mightier flow in Catania. We felt in the blackened streets its shroud of dread and contradiction. Most of the city consists of eighteenth-century edifices. It was wrecked in 1669 by a fiery tongue of lava that slid and pushed for more than eighteen miles from Etna and burned and buried part of the city. Then, in 1693, an earthquake leveled much of the center.

Given that the past in Italy is always physically present, there was an unconvincing optimism in the unified Baroque result undertaken to restore devastated Catania. Too much continuity and stucco in the eighteenth-century Baroque profile introduced a feeling of artificial theater to the whole of the center. Where were the other eras one expected in Italian cities? The blackness of the streets seemed an oppressive reminder. The empty plaster patches in walls in the cathedral itself, which had been stripped back to when the French of Aragon ruled, hinted at the destruction. The

gaps, joined to the Baroque solutions that filled in what had been lost, were just hopeless allusions to an invasion without end.

Catania, in its slightly morbid elegance, puts a face to the ambitious experiment that Italy has always been. By continuously committing to and extending habitations on land that is altered by earthquake and volcano, people (and the cities and villages they build) have challenged and often ignored the natural realities that have determined Italian history. Catania, because of what is missing in its urban story, suggests a fatalistic bravery as powerful as all the ups and downs of Italian politics, wars, and dominations. Metternich's famed statement that "Italy is only a geographic expression" is accurate. It would be thought-provoking if the "only" could be excised. To understand a unification of psyches from north to south, at least where, from ancient times onward, catastrophic earth events occurred, is to uncover a tested and elemental bond uniting a people who share this peninsula as a place of pleasure and unpredictable terror.

3

I took no volcanic rock from the landscape at Etna, or from the streets of Catania. I had not even seen a puff of smoke when I scanned Etna from Taormina, much less slurps of red molten fire. But I know earthquakes, another violent force shaping lives and history in Italy, firsthand. And earthquakes, far more than volcanoes, take disastrous tolls on human life. Earthquakes touch nearly everyone as a destabilizing element that shifts under the mountain chains and landmasses forming the peninsula. The tectonic plates shudder and rearrange often, sending fear and ripples of panic through villages and jolts through cities. Our house wheezes and groans about two or three times a year. The rattling chandeliers, the occasional broken vase have been, thus far, the worst results, but the sensation of the house dancing above its foundation does not leave the soles of one's feet for weeks.

In 2012, quite near our city, parts of several villages were reduced to near rubble. The death toll reached twenty. The number of people who found themselves one day living in tents in an area known for its wealth and efficiency—its adherence to building codes and knowledge of seismic activity—reached into the tens of thousands. The quakes and shocks continued for weeks and shook a profound sense of security in the residents of the province.

The recent deaths in the Emilian Po Plain are terrible periodic peaks in what seems to recur every few years: Somewhere in Italy, the earth trembles in a catastrophic shake. Poorly constructed schools heave in and crush an entire classroom of young children with pencils in their hands. Streets disappear; the cathedral dome cracks and the bell tower smashes to bits. Nearly 40 percent of Italians live on ground prone to quakes. The 1908 earthquake in Messina, which claimed eighty thousand lives, is the marker for devastation. While building codes have advanced and ways of measuring or predicting danger have progressed, lives on the peninsula continue to be literally thrown in the air, or undermined, as monuments, like the frescoes in Assisi, fall and people underneath die. Assisi's earthquake was followed by the world with the same intensity that the flood in Florence was. There were ten deaths, and each was a tragedy, but the heaps of broken plaster from the frescoes, including those of Giotto in the basilica, were the most striking images communicating the vulnerability of things of beauty to time.

In recent decades, there were 989 deaths in Friuli; in Irpinia, near Naples, nearly 3,000; in Aquila, an agonizing 323. These natural disasters, because of the importance of historical memory, perhaps because they are remembered not just from the last century but also from earlier centuries, conjure a collective memory that prevails about the power of nature and its lawless destruction of human life. Far more than serving as cautionary tales, admonishments for the enforcement of honest building practices, the presence of unstable forces in nature invariably reveals the uncertain odds of living. These stories put forth loss of life and property as nearly an inevitable consequence of government disorganization (eternal) and the fact that human beings will always remain vulnerable to the whims of ungovernable natural elements.

My mother-in-law, a schoolteacher who certainly had no spare time, gave up four weeks in the summer to live in a tent and cook for the earthquake victims living in tents in Friuli in 1976. She was in her late fifties by then. She responded to her memories of hunger and helplessness during World War II. A tent, a cold basin of water for washing, evenings spent warming up around an open fire, Mass under the trees—these were elements she recognized as part of emergencies and war and they didn't frighten her. Her religious faith encouraged her to involve herself in the suffering of others.

The government, naturally, is expected to intervene in natural disasters. The extent of the financial support is rarely bickered about. People agree that victims should be aided and compensated. Invariably, much money for these disasters mysteriously and tragically never reaches its destination. Yet the corruption rarely stirs rank rebellion. There is consensus—if not the actual means to carry through the reconstructions—that if funds disappear, more must be found, since people are entitled to compensation, even if it means a special, temporary tax. In the case of the most recent quake, a national two-cent tax has been added to gasoline.

Many conditions that my mother-in-law endured while she was in Friuli did not strike her as personally harsh. If beauty in life is to draw frosted patterns on a window, this is possible only if the room is without heat. The postcards that reached her for years afterward with little more than "Ciao" were sufficient thanks and signs that the mud, the despair, the wreckage from the earth's instability had been defeated.

"*Ciao.*"

"*Tutto bene.*"

"*Ciao, ancora.*"

"*Oggi e' bellissimo.*"

"Today, it's beautiful."

4

The Internet could provide much more information about earthquakes, but I don't want to fill pages with knowledge that has not been earned. So much put on pages now appears precisely because of these miraculous ways to locate new sources. This kind of facility for assembling what seems to add up to an authoritative picture, when in reality the topic has not been a subject of real study for the author, must have many implications. This method is still too recent, in my opinion, to assess its positive and negative meanings. But perhaps because words can add up, too smoothly, too soon, they lack the specific associations and integration that make a description more than information. It was experience and participation in a common cause, after all, that made my mother-in-law respond with such a deep offer of empathy.

Connectedness that comes from continuity and a sense of humanity takes time to establish and may include an identification with suffering. To understand how connectedness shapes the psyche is a way of reading the country. It probably is necessary to entertain a feeling for the word *connectedness*, without forcing what it means, before it can be understood as a central element here. Embedded in the magma of Christian messages about equality and poverty through the centuries in Italy, and the country's mid-twentieth-century political pact with universal social rights, are seeds and roots—however smashed, twisted, mutated they are—that probably have all left traces in that word, *connectedness*, and its concept of community. In the deep consciousness of people, there is a call for compassion and a mistrust of individualism that is most often perceived as narrow and heartless capitalism. In the magma is ancestral uncertainty, the unknown, which always proposes something collective as a corresponding truth.

In Pompeii—in the emotion of fatality generated by the unforgettable casts made from the impressions of people whose lives stopped in the ashes—a heartbreaking vision of life continues. In

the positions of bodies that express torment, life has outlasted life: the forever new that Keats attributes to the figures on the urn. Yet in Pompeii, the images that have lasted fix the opposite meaning of *new*. They immortalize a real place crushed by inexorable forces.

The city rests under everyone's eyelids and awakens when a national disaster strikes. Pompeii, the vast city where ashes fell for three days, hypnotizing and disbelieved, preserves a graphic chapter in history. Those perfect human bodies caught running, sleeping, and the cats and dogs curled up in what must have been choking shade, are ghosts. Fixed in their own time, they speak, not to give warnings but still appearing to breathe the normal life that had been going on: visits to the bread shop and the baths, the personal altars, the lane where horses were shod and men visited houses of ill repute. They face outward, transparent victims of nature, which can strike anyone, independent of class or beliefs.

XVII

Going South

Nothing is a greater epic than the sea.
>   —William Benjamin, in a review of Alfred Döblin's
>   *Berlin Alexanderplatz*

1

Years ago, family vacations took us to the Gargano Peninsula in Puglia, where we stayed in a modest hotel with its own beach of white sand, a few lounge chairs, and simple food that usually consisted of pasta with flavorful oil and tomatoes, and a slice of sheep's cheese or a few sardines for the second course. We reasoned that we were doing the right thing, eating in such a healthy way. Yet our stomachs growled.

The hotel had a fig tree that reached the second floor outside of our balcony. Before the early-rising owner began to tap the branches with a long stick, we had already skimmed off the ripe ones and eaten them. When the branches rustled and shook around eight, we felt a pang, but no more than that. Like peasants who had tricked their padrone, we felt in the right. The figs were delicious, filling, and warm. The owner had other fruit trees, and we were at odds with his justification for the stingy portions: his obligation to amass five dowries for his daughters. Once we were at home, like Pugliesi who move away and insist they could never live there again, we reminisced about what a special time it was. We extolled the virtues of Pasquale, the man who could never officially be called a lifeguard—no Red Cross certificate, no watchtower—who interpreted every sign the sea made. We remembered the enchanting, massive white cows that grazed at the far edge of the beach and the water that sparkled like aquamarines. We blushed about compensatory visits to a *pasticceria* where, each time, we consumed a kilo of marzipan sweets. We returned to Vieste every summer for as long as our daughter would go with us.

Now we were going back to Puglia, after a gap of twenty years. We were meeting friends in Bari. Our motive was their grandchild's baptism in a city central to early Christianity and later to the Byzantine Church. Once the baby was baptized and we celebrated with a week of being together, my husband and I planned a series of stops before returning north. I wanted to see places I had visited in the sixties, as well as track the social problem of illegal immigrants. No southern region knows better than Puglia the realities of immigration and invasions, bordered as it is on two sides by the Adriatic and Ionian Seas.

The way southern Italians have been invaded from the sea and ruled by foreigners and corrupt administrations, as well as the fact that Phoenicians, Mycenaeans, and Greeks began settling in significant numbers more than four thousand years ago, contribute to a different narrative from the one that holds sway in the north. The sun plays a different part in life when barriers are canceled by the sea. Winds—the sirocco, mistral, and bora—play different parts. There is a slower pace, and the word *ancient* comes to mind because of the presence of natural elements that still sup-

port a way of life that is as old as the Neolithic. This life of open
sea, sun, and wind has influenced the history of what is known as
the Mezzogiorno, the heel and toe of Italy's boot.

2

I have lots of memories of the south in the late sixties and early
seventies: the Rome years and those immediately following. I remember the tension of being in Naples when cholera broke out.
The crowded, already slightly menacing streets took on an extra
edge that made me feel frightened of being touched by a germ. I
remember young kids begging when our two-horsepower Citroën
stopped at lights and that many of the small, dirty hands held
stones they threatened to throw through the windshield.

The eighteenth-century Neapolitan philosopher Giambattista Vico was known to me because James Joyce had used his
theories in structuring *Finnegans Wake*. By the time I lived in
Rome, I was very fond of the learned Neapolitan who had provided me with a rich complement to Cartesian arguments for rationalism. Vico described how life could be lived to include civic
values while maintaining a wider focus. Since truth was never
determined outside of a mind, which carried with it culture and
assumptions, fuller consciousness was the goal of society.

"The truth itself is made." Human concerns, which were not
the same as empirical observations or axioms, were part of understanding how to live. History was but a long spiral of epochs
repeating themselves. There was the period of the gods (the metaphor of the Divine), the heroic age with its idealized figures, and
then the human, which referred to periods of democracy, where,
by applying reason and the senses, humanity was slowly cor-
rupted and slipped back into barbarism. Thus began again the
cycle of looking for the supernatural. The three epochs wound like
a spiral that repeated a new version of the old archetypal patterns.

3

In Pizzo Calabro, in Reggio Calabria, part of the toe of Italy's Mediterranean coast, I spent a summer in the early seventies doing archaeology. In order for us to rent the house that a Calabrian family was building, the numerous family members sheltered in their unfinished basement. But they preferred to spend their time in a hut on the beach. At night, the sea breeze turned cold. The family built a small fire for warmth and, especially, light. If there were projects like washing clothes, they built a larger one. Daily meals were prepared on the fire; food was preserved on the fire, as well: Piles of tomatoes were boiled and stirred in an iron vat for a full day, until they were reduced to a thick paste. The sauce was sealed in Coke bottles and fruit-juice bottles scavenged from the beaches. These hundreds of odd glass jars of preserves were the basis of variety through the winter.

If the fire was large, it was started once the sun had dropped. Faces marked by dramatic shadows and lit by continuous explosions of burning sap cinders were animated around the iron kettle. Men and women took turns completing tasks while the moon shone its bright path on the waves. Sometimes the family worked straight through the night, sorting scrap metal, bundling groups of sticks, while the lamps of the fishermen bobbed far out in the dark. Sometimes they were still talking at sunrise as the fishermen dragged their boats to shore.

I remember translating and writing letters to people in the United States for a few of their neighbors, who had reading glasses but could not read or write. I remember a surplus of pastry shops because so many men had worked on big liners and returned home to set up bakeries. There were too many for any of them to make a proper living. The south, plagued today by unemployment rates that are nearly twice those of the north, reflects initiative, where futility must not be considered. After I write this down, I immediately want to take the sentence back. I want to polish the attribute into a positive, unambiguous quality. Like lizards that stop for a second before darting for a dark fissure, statements about the differences in mentality and conditions in the north and different regions in the south seem fleeting and cannot adequately express this distinct atmosphere.

Along the autostrada going toward Bari, where our friends' granddaughter's baptism was to take place, many bleached hills gleamed with terraced installations of solar panels. Windmills and their loud turbine sounds shot up often: noisy flocks of widely spaced propellers with candy cane–striped bases. The Pugliesi have been quick to harness new sources of energy and income. The Lega Nord, the Northern League, with a constituency of about 12 percent of Italian voters, has built much of its platform on stereotyping the south as unfairly subsidized and parasitic. The windmills and solar panels all along the highway announced that the south has intentions of using its abundant natural resources for ecological progress.

Yet in cities and villages in Puglia, there were more people using canes than in any place I have seen in the north. More people seem to limp; perhaps they are not offered hip replacements on the national health plan. Adult children, with noticeable birth defects, trudge along, holding the arms of relatives. Prices for things

were half of those in the north. The most heavenly peaches, a bulging bag of nine pounds, cost only a euro. Who could feel that pittance was a fair price as she paid it to a man who, while not old, was as weathered as a worn burlap sack?

Most narration in Puglia goes back to that man, someone who is not old but is brutally or relentlessly worn-out. In the centuries of stories, there are the myriad landowners, the absentee owners, the foreign governments, the tyrants and the Pugliesi, those who stay and those who leave to find work. The rhythm is there in the seas and in the tales told by Greeks. Theirs is not the story of Genova or Venice, of the finding of new worlds and capitalizing on them. Theirs is the *Odyssey*, the single man, the setting out and the return, and the Penelope who waits, weaving and unweaving her tapestry, in boredom, nervousness, or, like the sea itself, an epic about passing time.

The stories in the south, from Naples to Palermo to Lecce, mix folk wisdom from darkness and poverty, myths from the Greeks, the Arabs, messages from Christianity and the Byzantine world, as well as notions of government left by the Norman conquerors, and the rapacious, absentee Bourbons from Spain. The tales in one way are about hardships. In another, they are about possibilities for the soul. In Puglia, the recent epoch of the human has often been about the sadness and sorrow of getting work and then paying part of every paycheck for the rest of one's life to the person who procured the job. In the epoch of the human, in the nets of bribes and reprisals, obstacles seem to be systemic, and in order to survive psychologically, southerners turn back to the epoch of metaphor and the supernatural, the epoch of the gods.

4

Our friends' grandchild was to be baptized in Bari on a Tuesday. Her parents had organized it beautifully and the symbolism was strong. Growing older, I'm hardly alone in worrying about how we can build a compassionate sense of community. Even if we are not monsters, it is undoubtedly useful, perhaps imperative, to reckon with our own sense of culpability. Assuming superiority in a system of profit with minimal social obligations; starting wars that ask soldiers who do not even know where the enemy country is on a map to sacrifice their lives; destroying our environment at a speed never before known in history—these are sobering realities that we are complicit in. Baptism, which admits original sin, a concept that seemed unbearably unfair when I was a child trying to understand how religion worked, I now find symbolically rich. Unconsciousness is our original state. Consciousness of the mystery of life, the existence of good and evil as well as the infinity of love, is a powerful hope.

In our week together, while the household was still asleep, I crept outside to savor my favorite time of day. Sitting on a drywall, I usually followed the sunlight inching across the lawn and into olive trees and watched butterflies landing on the lavender. The olive trees seemed identical to those bleached-bark swirls in Antonio Ligabue's paintings or Van Gogh's last visions.

The inky nights, when we sat on the roof of the *trullo*—a cone-shaped stone house painted white, with steps that traditionally lead up to a flat place to sit—silence settled on us as we chatted. The winds on the roof carried a chill. Slowly, we stopped talking. How could those brilliant handfuls of light be understood as fires and explosions and who knows what else that we had no notion of whatsoever? Being conscious of the sky is an experience that I rarely enjoy for more than a few minutes in the city. Full moon, half-moon. Glances or remarks. Crawling down the narrow steps from the roof, I was unable to make them out, so I leaned against the cool wall. Even the darkness on the stairs, such an insignificant sensation of darkness, made me feel glad to touch the grass with bare feet. Yet, having gotten lost in the sweeping sparkle of the sky, the unlit path to the house seemed almost more lonely to me.

5

Carlo Levi's book *Christ Stopped at Eboli* awakened English-speaking readers, as well as Italians, to southern poverty; well into the early seventies, some people in regions like Basilicata and Puglia were still living in calcareous caves and coexisting with animals in order to keep warm in the colder months. The Eboli in Levi's book was the last train stop when he was sent as an anti-Fascist internal exile to Basilicata in 1935. Ten years later, he recounted the lives there; in one chapter, he gives details of life in the town of Matera, with its over twenty thousand cave dwellers. *I sassi*, as the caves are called in Italian, became images of a way of life that had persisted for at least ten thousand years.

Natural structures, without running water and sanitation systems, the disease-infested *sassi* offended a country with a new constitution and a plan for modernization that included using television to teach literacy. Italy, during the economic miracle of the sixties, was lifted into a new experience of itself. One reaction was to try to eliminate the realities of poverty that made people fundamentally unequal and unable to join the twentieth century. It meant breaking the sharecropping agricultural model.

When I first visited Matera, in the late sixties, it was still partially inhabited. The impression of proximity, people who could hear each other night and day, the roughness of stone windows with no glass, curtains that were doors, the sounds and smells of hundreds of families living together—these did not strike me as horrifying then, even if Levi had considered their state "absolute wretchedness." His passionate observations referred to the town he saw in 1935. Something of my life in the courtyard scaled what I saw. The filth and absolute despair were not obvious, although conditions were difficult, beginning with limited sanitation. I could grasp a few familiar elements: neighbors who saw into each other's rooms, who shouted and shared. Yet, still inhabited, the caves seemed at least to shelter dwellers from the brutalities of weather

and provided means to form a hivelike organization that helped them face many survival problems. There were cars by then, which could take up some of the food and wood that otherwise would still have been hoisted by mules and on human backs. The conditions for solidarity and survival overlapped and were elaborated. The caves also provided a scenic overview of the valley: The position from on high offered fine vistas.

Revisiting Matera, I had not expected the darkened structures to give off the impression of a deserted prison. Not a murmur from the lives of the twenty thousand people who had animated them. They had long since been transferred to modern housing on the outskirts of town. Empty sockets of interconnected limestone held an eerie sense of atrocity and shame. A few caves had been turned into luxury hotels. A way of sheltering that lasted longer than any standing cathedral had been transformed for a certain number of tourists into a strange, chic experience.

For many centuries, the people in the caves did not live much better than animals, but there is evidence that they found other dimensions to develop. They had figured out how to form groups and, when needed, they organized to resist the landowners and conquerors who ruled over them. Life was brutal and difficult: The

occupants worked on the land, cultivating it, while barely having enough to eat because the padrone took the fruits of their labor. Byzantine monks occupied the *sassi* for several centuries, and cave churches were built from rock formations. The spirit of holding out against nobles, Normans, Spanish, and Mafia presences was still part of their identity when the cave dwellers in Matera became the first community in Italy to resist the invading Wehrmacht. Poverty had not made them helpless or meek.

Pasolini filmed his story of the Gospel of Saint Matthew there when people still remembered vibrations in the caves: the times when they could hear each other making love or fighting or beating water out of clothes. When they were no longer domestic dwellings, Mel Gibson shot his violent movie of Christ's crucifixion there. The caves and their occupants had become props.

6

In Alberobello and as far as the eye could see on the roads leading to the *trullo*, in which we stayed, were olive trees older than three or four centuries. They were figures and shapes born from fairy tales and myths—some shaggy as hairy giants; some bent, with branches springing out like orators; some with roots that split like hooves with huge nails. Not one was like another. Efforts to keep them alive with crutches, infusions, amputations, grafts were visible all along the dusty roads.

Olive trees offer a crop but are a special form of farming. They are about paradise lost and human beings, who, having fallen from grace and been cast out, must find ways to survive. The olive trees, olive orchards, olive forests, the long stretches of bushy, twisting trees, are an ancient language that belongs to Vico's era of the gods. The trees, with their gifts of precious oil, ask for as much patience as do the tiny black olives that require so much work. The ancient trunks are waves of heaving bark, swirled and cracked as if fires had exploded them. People who cultivate olives have a pastoral relationship to them, like shepherds. The trees' value, as producers, has been supplemented by the addition of new trees. In social and genetic terms, the shaggy, twisted ones remain elders, relics, factotums. They populate fields like folk shrines. Emanating

magic and swaying their dust-green leaves like spirits, they embody the model for a way of life.

Ulysses built his marriage bed from a rooted olive tree, and in Penelope's last test, she says she will bring the marriage bed. He reproaches her, since their bed cannot be moved from where it grows in their house. The olive tree in Puglia goes back, marked by the presences of Greeks, who were able to coexist and intermarry with local populations without the wars that the Romans brought, without the annihilation and superimposition of culture. The Greeks came to Puglia, to the ports along the Adriatic, and left their genes and their way of life starting around 800 B.C.E.

7

Puglia, although it has largely updated its physical structures since the sixties, when I first visited, still lacks the economic successes of the north for many reasons. In some places, almost half of its

young people are unemployed. Puglia and other southern regions know the reality of out-migration. The southerners who move away leave a sense of desolation in the more isolated villages, and yet they also bring an acceptance of change to those who stay behind. The attitude of generosity and social graciousness characterizes the little villages and the cities in ways that still perplex the children and grandchildren of relatives who emigrated for more economic opportunity. Many say that they cannot imagine living at the pace that people in these villages do, and yet, like us returning to the hotel in the Gargano, almost everyone admits that the life—the food, the *passeggiate*, the celebrations, the weddings, all accompanied by the transparent sea—makes them feel more than ordinary guests. They are welcomed into a fabric of community.

8

I was anxious to reach Metaponto, a brief drive to the western coast of the Ionian Sea. I remembered the museum as a source for the subject I was interested in: immigration and cultural assimilation. The impact and reality of both are documented in the glass cases of the museum there. Early objects capture movement and exchanges between cultures that were well defined by around 1600 B.C.E. Cultures considered part of the Bronze Age, and some with local attributions, like the Messapii, are shown to have intermarried, especially going forward in time, with the Greeks. The region's history exemplifies the various effects of cross-culture: examples of integration, subjugation, and periods when culture becomes a new blend.

As the sea brings Spartans across the Adriatic into Puglia, you can follow, in the remains of material culture—vases, vessels, jewelry—the way Greek myths were absorbed. Epeius, the supposed builder of the Trojan horse, was said to be from Metaponto. The workshop in which he is said to have built the horse assumes importance because it lets the locals enter the Greek story. Vases telling Greek myths become items produced by locals who have learned vase painting from Greeks who immigrated especially for that purpose. In the glass cases, objects tell of women's lives and men's lives through combs, pins, hooks, knives, kettles. Burial customs show mentalities blending. Pythagoras fled to Metaponto to escape taking a position in a local war near Bari. He became a teacher. Greek temples like the ones to Hera and Apollo stand on surrounding hills and were used by Romans and Christians later on.

I kept the large museum entry ticket illustrating stages of life. The first was birth, followed by myth, war, work, games, luxury, the beyond, and immortality. Those categories bleed through to life in the present. Even graffiti in that part of the world express a philosophical turn of mind. Instead of the spasms of enthusiasm—"*Giulia, ti amo*"—or curses against ethnic groups spray-painted on walls in the northern city in which I live, I found poetry on walls in Puglia. In Polignano, a quote from Tasso, "All time not spent in love is wasted," and on stairs there, a translation of Walter Benjamin: "Nothing is a greater epic than the sea." Many words used in graffiti are written in Greek. There is culture and dialogue in these fleeting observations that sweeten daily lives. Here, if we stop, we have perceived something that aids us in understanding a feature of the differences between north and south, even if, like a nimble lizard, it will soon dive into a spot where it can no longer be scrutinized.

9

The history of Puglia over the past four thousand years began to take shape in my mind, especially in the museum. I realized how differently I had understood the very same cities when I visited them more than forty years earlier. Then everything was filtered through an earnest but far less focused mind and heart. Often I saw what I wanted to see and was thrilled by difference. When I returned to Puglia, what I saw in the remains of civilizations was that the truths residing in them were basically opaque.

I did not have Keats's feeling of nostalgia for time stopped on the urn. I was interested in the little bit of truth that lay in the hands of the makers, the ones who spun the potters' wheels, the lives that had to think through and accept the Greek myths that were new to them. Those traces, if they existed at all, were to be found in the living people in Puglia. I thought about the farmers, and how grain and grapes still grew. I thought even more about the silences that surround objects once people die.

The evidence in the museum cases showed ideas about culture that varied. There were cases showing the objects introduced

by conquerors, sweeping out what had come before. There were cases that showed objects that were the results of cultural mixing and borrowing. The context for all was the one on the ticket: birth to immortality.

Our world is undergoing rapid change as cultures penetrate one another without knowing much about each other. Three-quarters of our brain is mapped for responses of fear, anger, and aggression. The need to survive dominates our mind's circuits. The ratio for the brain's responses must have been more or less the same then as now. If such different results were obvious in less than forty vitrines, why isn't it easier to grasp the idea of rejecting force and accepting time, adaptation, the gradual borrowing of ideas?

Taking a photo of a stunning Roman mirror, with a goddess as the stem, my face appeared in the reflection on the glass case in the museum, and thus, for a moment, superimposed, I became the face in the mirror. In a land of signs, where snakes are considered omens, I noted, with a touch of ironic pleasure, the overlapping image had placed me as a presence among those varied responses.

10

When we reached Manduria, an inland city that had its own Messapian ruins, I finally had arrived at the place where I hoped to explore the problem of refugees. Manduria held more than two thousand recent refugees in a controversial tent village. The location of the camp was kept vague, like many of the previous sites we had been seeking. People said it was too far out of town to be reached. Beyond the city proper, I saw a horizontal line of blue in the middle of a deserted field, far from the road. To its right were buildings for carabinieri. Immigrant arrivals in one form or another have always been a part of the south's legacy from the sea. These North Africans had entered Italy illegally through the faraway island of Lampedusa, south of Sicily. They paid to be piled

on boats, crossings usually organized by criminals. Many boats arrived with some or most passengers half-dead.

A word was spray-painted on a brick wall near the road. The blue letters read *"Insicurezza"*: Insecurity. One word. No implicit racist hate in the mind that left it for contemplation. The noun expressed a human feeling, and, given that it was only one word, it was ambiguous. Insecurity might refer to the illegal refugees, most so desperate by the time they arrive that they need to be not only taken in but given medical treatment. More plausibly, insecurity describes the feelings of residents of Manduria since social upheavals in Libya and uprisings in Tunisia unleashed another wave of immigration. The refugees rushed into a country that is already estimated to harbor more than one million illegal immigrants.

I'd read that many of the refugees, who had been bused from Lampedusa, arrived in batches of five or six hundred in one or two days. Many had taken the opportunity to escape during the hours of confusion when busloads that arrived simultaneously had to be unloaded and registered. Local residents living close to the camp had been terrified by escapees running through their yards. Some Tunisians, who perhaps numbered seven hundred (their exact number will remain unknown, since they had not been counted), began running as soon as the bus doors opened. It is thought that at least one hundred escaped as the first hundred were being checked in. "What should I do," asked the guard rhetorically as he was interviewed about the problem. "Do you expect me to shoot them?"

Do you expect me to shoot them? is a shocking question, worthy of Socrates and of his careful examination of the logic leading to definitions of justice and ideas about a republic. In the guard's question—which is, in part, rhetorical irony and anger, and, in part, a far deeper demand—a southern root lies exposed. The camp guard expresses a common statement of personal exaspera-tion and resentment about the human considerations that are often overlooked by laws themselves or the corrupt applications of them. This guard rejects organization so poor that he is expected to enforce it by use of violent oppression. He is a close companion to the clerk in Rome who wrote my request for work. He claims as part of his identity a sympathy with the oppressed.

The buses will keep coming in chaotic ways and the people who have workable legs will continue to run. The perception of public systems is such that it is difficult for many people in Bari or Manduria to simply project what's wrong in their lives onto for-eign immigrants. How can chaos be handled if it is perceived? How can violence be handled if people know and remember the results of violence, wars, cruelty, and submission? The immigrants are by no means innocents—not all of them at least. Many have paid criminals in order to come. Many are criminals themselves. But many are normal people, women and children and men, willing to work, even if they arrive half-dead and without papers.

Chaos has been unleashed in ports like Lampedusa and Bari, and in places like the tent villages going up in Manduria. Some problems are practical: How to sort out people who cannot stay, how to determine what to do with those who must find other cit-ies, people who often had no intention of immigrating to Italy but only hoped to land and then be sent on to their families in France or Belgium? How can TB, parasites, and AIDS be screened? How can periods for processing arrivals be shortened when rumors say that Manduria will receive another two or three thousand people who must be held until they can be registered?

Life in the wide-open fields of recently erected blue tents, only partially governed by laws that perhaps the immigrants, the townspeople, and the police officials all interpret in different ways, is a problem that has existed in cities like Bari and Taranto for as long as there have been cities and the sea. In fame and fact, the Mafia has deep holds over the south, but the reality is that most people live their lives operating under gestures of tolerance, common sense, and a specific compassion for people facing hardship. "Would you expect me to shoot someone who is trying to escape?"

A general in the carabinieri told me that immigrants who are illegal are a problem because at least a third of them are criminals in their own countries and they come knowing that the Italian justice system is so weak that even if they are apprehended, their chances of being released are very great. But how does one decide as a man jumps over a fence if he is a criminal or not? Perhaps he is just a human being hoping to hide in the woods and reach relatives, counting on luck and periods when there is an amnesty and briefly people can be legalized.

Puglia has legalized many immigrants. They are entering, usually with sponsorships, by supporting the domestic responsibilities of life and prosperity—taking care of old people and keeping them in their homes; taking care of children for parents who work. The illegal workers do farm labor, picking fruit and vegetables. The sea keeps delivering more people, most recently those fleeing war in North Africa, people without papers. In 2011, they arrived in numbers ten times greater than in the previous year. More than fifty thousand reached Italy at Lampedusa. Twenty thousand were recorded and received as political refugees. Figures on the rest are not available.

Risks are enormous, even before landing. In 2011, more than two thousand people hoping to reach Italy drowned at sea. Recently, only fifty of two hundred men, women, and children were rescued off the shore of Lampedusa, once their small, tragically overcrowded boat capsized. The boats and ships packed with impoverished, desperate passengers are a biblical spectacle. The Polish poet Wisława Szymborska begins her poem "Children of Our Age" with these lines:

We are children of our age.
It's a political age.

All day long, all through the night,
all affairs—yours, ours, theirs—
are political affairs.

Whether you like it or not,
your genes have a political past,
your skin, a political cast,
your eyes, a political slant.

Whatever you say reverberates,
whatever you don't say speaks for itself.
So either way you're talking politics.

Even when you take to the woods,
you're taking political steps
on political grounds.

(Translated by Stanisław Barańczak
and Clare Cavanagh)

11

Our last night was spent in Ortona over the border in Abruzzo.
The city, which was still a secondary port, had been bombed
heavily in World War II. Many buildings, including the cathedral,
had been reconstructed using new bricks. Thirteen hundred civil-
ians had died in raids that offered few chances to escape from the
falling bombs. The harbor, with its fascinating cranes and machines, tugboats and railroad lines, was busy, and ships carrying
freight were docking. It was still a working city, a city that used
the sea as a place to find work. Signs of damage from World War II
remained, while the fortified castle built in a war against the Turks

in the fifteenth century had become a magnificent promenade and tourist spot from which to view the sea.

I pulled open my windows at five the next morning to see the sun appearing in nearly orange increments. A mutt sniffed along the boardwalk, followed by a woman biking back bread. A yellow crane was not yet swinging to hoist its first load from a freighter. The sea was neither up nor asleep. It was there—far different from what we call ancient—canceling, while bringing the tide in. The way it wrinkles, storms, and smoothes out in such tranquillity or tumult along the land, it is too deep to give way to human whim. Who could imagine its presence as other than a silent interrogation? How could rationalism and technology have more power in defining culture than what the sea decrees to the people who live by its motions? While the sun rose, the soft indentations and ripples moving across its surface caught the light for a while and suggested why feelings, the overpowering authority especially of feelings—those of acceptance, if not precisely resignation—hold such sway. The sea expresses and stretches out in a rhythm like the heart, which operates on its own.

XVIII

Antonella

The finder cannot unsee once it has been seen.

—Vladimir Nabokov, *Speak, Memory*

THE OTHER SIDE OF THE TIBER

1

I had not really thought about Antonella, a young woman from Sardinia who lived in the house attached to mine in the courtyard, until I started working on these reflections. My memory, having reopened the door to my Rome years, started to let people and their meanings cast mute shadows where previously they had rested, completely out of sight. Although most memories flow away, some remain with qualities that are anything but fluid. Some have nearly schistlike sparkle and others suddenly feel like stains.

My neighbor Antonella brings up themes of female equality and very slow progress. In Italy each year, violent crimes are repeatedly committed against women. The range of subjects about women and violence covered on the front page of today's paper is no exception. A husband has murdered his wife in a fit of jealousy, killing their two children and the third, whom she was carrying in her womb. This horrifying event follows an article on the same page about Sakineh, a woman condemned for adultery and sentenced to be stoned to death in Iran. Still on the same page are critical comments about Colonel Gadhafi, who has just completed a state visit in which he paid two hundred young Italian women to attend three days of seminars on Islam. He announced that they would be treated with far more respect in Libya than in their own country. This unleashed from the Left and the Right, and from women's groups of all positions, a vehement protest at the comparison. Many of the young girls who accepted the invitation

hoped to be interviewed on TV and, in their low-cut tops and miniskirts, spotted by talent scouts.

Women in Italy dominate many sectors, although they lag far behind in executive positions and professorial ones. Often their rates of graduation from university exceed those of men by 15 or 20 percent. The national health system offers mammograms and Pap smears as routine regular exams. Yet the historical context for women continues to suggest an inevitability about the difference in social conditions. Women are burdened with many assumed roles. Domestic violence, while now not completely ignored, is still prevalent in heterosexual relationships. But it is irrefutable that consciousness surrounding the topic has changed fundamentally.

Women's rights have been enunciated, beginning with the right to divorce, decided in a public referendum in 1974. Society continues to extend the rights of families in terms of help for young children. The feminist may sniff at this and insist it proves prejudice about women's roles. Yet most mothers and fathers, if they have children, would agree that financial support, however minimal, and protecting jobs during domestic leaves, benefits them personally and also the society at large. Families are given up to a year of paid maternity leave, and the right to nurture is considered a central piece of identity. Women cannot lose their jobs because of maternity, nor can they be forced to return, for up to two years. The priority of paid leave (most commonly five months) is social leveling. Many who would not otherwise have the means to take time off or hire help are able to assist their young children. The right is also given to men who want to assume the role of primary caregiver, to those who adopt, and it extends as well to cases of foster care, so that foster parents can stay at home to stabilize a child's start in life. The latest government statistics, however, show that women in families work seven twenty-hour days each week. The low birth rate—9.2 children per 1,000—reflects this.

The undisguised levels of prostitution in Italy, shocking to an Anglo-Saxon mind, are a generally accepted reality, at least at the conversational level. Prostitution is shrugged off, sometimes rationalized as an obvious resource for women who have no other means of support. This view is offered for street women and also, in the recent years of Italy's degraded political climate, extended to those young women who wish to enter high-paying careers in entertainment and even government. In the years of rampant sexual scandals, a ferocious cynicism among young women, as well as men, framed sexual favors as an acceptable private transaction. This distancing is not reflected in the attitudes of the average person, who, after making certain that he or she will not be seen as a moralist who judges another's private behavior, will say that the general level of public morality needs to be lifted.

2

Antonella was stabbed by her husband around ten at night in the summer, when windows are left open like panting tongues. Fights in the yard and in the houses were common. Because of the loose view of privacy, along with the high volume of TV, it often felt as if all the explosions were taking place in my living room. Antonella's fights with her husband had been heard for some time—jagged and frightening. They were frightening because, as the courtyard members knew, they had no way of convincing Antonella that she was in danger.

The concept of disturbing the peace, which often calls out police in American suburbs, was foreign to the courtyard. A group of rock musicians practiced in the cellar underneath Rosina's room. They were young men who considered themselves heirs to the Rolling Stones. I struggled with them for the three years they played during hours when I was trying to write. But for the court-yard in general, I was a fanatic—a Roman category applied to anyone who holds a line.

"*Che fa-na-tica*," they would say to me when I asked for their support.

Che fa-na-tica—what obsessiveness. They are just boys having fun.

The musicians, who were nice but uninspired, often playing monotonous passages for hours, were certain of their immunity. Thus I remained unarmed, without any possibility of convincing them to accept limits on their playing. I made a series of uncertain stands that caused them to remind me, several times a week, of my fanaticism. No one in the yard would have ever called the police to settle such a dispute. Just as people on the road flash their lights to signal fellow drivers of the presence of police ahead, the musicians were a part of the yard's communal makeup and so were protected. A source of complaint, occasional fights, a chronic head-ache, they were part of the extended family nevertheless. Only at night did a fraying group, who wanted to watch TV, ask for a cease-fire.

"*Basta.*"

"*Basta* to you, too."

"*Basta*, I said."

Silence.

Then someone like Antonio would start honking his sax.

"*Baaaasta.*"

Silence.

Another note or two.

"*Baaaasta,*" Minica said.

"*Basta,*" shouted Signor Rolle.

Silence.

"*Va bene.*"

"*Buona notte.*"

Then, one quick, halfhearted drumroll to prove the band couldn't be pushed around.

3

Yet screams that sound like someone is being murdered are something entirely different. That night, Antonella let out a scream and then shouted that the knife had gone in. I had no phone, but Minica called the police and they came. Antonella's husband was taken, kicking and swearing, down the steps of their house and then Antonella left with another policeman, who took her to the hospital. As she left the courtyard, with people in all the windows, she lifted her bloodstained hands and said that he was a *coglione*, a worthless bag of testicles. That was her condemning conclusion.

Looking at some photos of Antonella—with her broad shoulders, coarse black hair, and two small children—I can almost bring back those days following his arrest. Antonella cooled off, although her tongue was always sharp and full of blasphemies. She still wore her bandage, which was close to the main artery in her neck, but began saying her cuts were nothing much. He had not put the knife in very deep. She began to worry about her situation were he not to come back. If prison took him away, and took his salary as a waiter, where would she be? Those in the courtyard, from Minica to Rosina, even including the furniture workers who were often so uselessly sarcastic, held tight to the opinion that Antonella was better off without him.

I was both surprised and pleased to be inside of the discussions, in which there was little disagreement. The courtyard had common sense about it, and, in its circular way of thinking, a fair amount of foresight. Much of the daily bickering was not hostility, but boredom. In this case, there was a remarkable unity that drew upon deep memories of violence and of where Antonella might end up should she forget that her life and her children's lives were in danger.

Rosina was frightened by the stabbing. She pulled her shutters nearly closed for most of the days immediately afterward. But she listened behind them, and her voice would come out, disembodied but bell-like: "No, no, you must send him away. Do you understand? Send him away." Then, as if the cloud of danger needed to be dispelled, without missing another breath, she would pick up the Rosary where she had left off: "The Lord is with thee. Blessed art thou among women, and blessed is the fruit of thy womb, Jesus."

In the end, Antonella's husband waited in jail for a few months. Antonella took in a temporary boarder. The fighting, although domestic, was of another sort. The boarder ate too much. Didn't pay bills. And the courtyard had new material to cast opinions on. Antonella, eventually, though, like me, left the courtyard, telling Minica that she was returning to her husband and Sardinia. There was a lack of confidence in her own worth, or a fatalism that made setting out on a new path more frightening than the terrible lot she had.

Federico Fellini, in *La Strada*, shows how tragically that attitude conditioned poor women, and how believable it was in the first half of the twentieth century in Italy. Giulietta Masina, as Gelsomina, cannot imagine any way of life other than her place in the traveling circus, where she will go back to the beatings and subjugations she knows under Zampanò. Antonella did not see a future outside of the role she knew, and she had no idea of economic independence. That was decades ago. Yet far too many examples of psychological subjugation persist, even when the climate for breaking those bonds has become more supportive.

As I write about Antonella, I am surprised by how naturally that violence was foreseen and how it was assumed, not only by Antonella but by the rest of us in the yard, to be nearly unavoidable. Antonella was a strong woman, but she was also stubborn. It was assumed that she lacked the ability to bend sufficiently to adapt to her life and that her attitudes would bring trouble down on her head. That particular form of fatalism, a strong conditioning combined with a lack of support systems and alternatives, is eye-opening when one must apply it to oneself.

When I lived in the yard, the inevitability of violence was still a notion projected onto people of poorer social classes. The idea of violence in the middle class, especially abuse of women or children, has been only slowly admitted and brought to light. For far too long, abuse was perceived as a source of shame and, therefore, a reality to be hidden. From the standpoint either of victims or of perpetrators, violence, in general, still has not been talked about enough. Physical and psychological violence is life-threatening and can deform anyone of either sex.

4

My capacity to float in the courtyard, joining in, while having a whole other life potentially waiting in another place, finally brought me to make the decision to go back into my first marriage. What expectations were, what duty was, our hubristic, unreal plans for roles for men and women who aspired to be artists—all this cannot really be summed up by my present view of those years or even of my own nature. I certainly had no sense of impatience and objectivity when it came to facing my contradictions. I pursued what I called love, and that was often intensity. The romanticism around the meaning of attraction and the intoxication of sharing intellectual ideas can't be put into words now, because the attitudes toward women, the narratives, the supporting structures have changed so drastically. I cannot, in honesty, explain my decision, except by saying that I wanted to do it.

What is telling, however, is that I decided to put the part about my leaving the courtyard in the chapter on Antonella. In theory, it could have waited until nearly the book's end. But when I recalled Antonella, I felt a vibration of my own that was too powerful to overlook. What appears like a stain in my memory, something I rarely remember, is that there had been violence in my marriage, violence and that blindness that made danger seem as if it were not real. Instead of backing off from it, not accepting it, I reached the terrible conclusion that I lacked courage if I walked away. I had spoken to people in my family and others about it, and there had not been even as much as the courtyard members' concerns about danger, except from a young man who cared so much, he offered to buy me a ticket back to the States. His mother asked me to consider leaving my marriage. She advised me to see a psychologist and then to let go.

My mother, instead, for three years urged me to go back. I am not moved at such a distance to spell out details. But I had also been molested, more than once as a child, and had been told, like many other unlucky girls with conforming mothers, never to speak of it. That dark muffling, which can seem so insignificant, given all that takes place in childhood, has come up now.

5

There was a climate in the times and certainly in our house that denied women autonomy, approval, and support for expression.

There was something that to this day I can only describe as unsettling in a formality that made niceness and optimism into a standard that was a kind of enforced censorship. No raised voices. No fights among the siblings. None of our friends was allowed to come to the house for a meal, an overnight. My parents did not entertain. So isolation was quite extensive and made it difficult to establish perspective on things. My mother, who was probably quite social, turned to me. Her inappropriate and dramatic stories of early loves, where she refused her suitors one after another until she was nearly raped; the man who went off to war and died, sending his belongings to my grandmother, with a note saying that my mother's rejection had made him enlist; her descriptions of where my father kissed her—these embarrassed and assaulted a gawky girl with horn-rimmed glasses. As I continued to grow, my mother's intrusions extended into my diary, my drawers, my desk. She proposed hormone shots to stunt my height. She pounced on me before I turned fourteen. "I want to give you a nose job for your birthday. There's no need for you to suffer." I was stunned that a nose that bore great resemblance to my father's was now targeted by her need to correct. My resistance, passive and otherwise, finally led her to cut my hair in my sleep. On it went. I protested this by quietly shaving off my eyebrows. In good family form, no one ever asked what had happened to them.

Although I would not have made the association with Antonella then, I do now. I was unable to listen and respond to the right advice. And although violence was a connection when I linked it to my return to a marriage, the violence in the relationship with my mother is what appears more fundamental. Like Antonella, in different degrees, I was missing awareness of basic elements that would have showed me how to strike a claim for my existence. I lived in many ways in my imagination, which provided lots of space for creative things that interested me and did not suggest that I discover the confidence I lacked. Time in subtle and aggressive ways has insisted that I do so.

6

Although I prepared to leave the courtyard, I kept the flat for some more years. I did, as the clerk hoped, have writing to show. I had used the years to write a novel. In the first months of my escape to Rome, the technical college in Oxford had invited me to return, but I had been certain that I would be better off as a writer if I stayed in Rome. Driven by an image of artists as people who must renounce and risk, I let that large piece of security go, lightly, without realizing I would never experience that level of professional or financial security again.

Long before I read Czesław Milosz, or Milan Kundera, or W. G. Sebald, and decades before gratefully reading Grace Paley, Denise Levertov, Meena Alexander, or Zadie Smith, I arrived at my own form of writing using cross-culture, a point of view constructed from fragments and tension. Part sociological interviews, part fiction, my novel reproduced the courtyard; one piece was created by inventing Rosina's and Minica's and Marcello's lives and a plot; and the other part, which alternated with the fictional chapters, presented interviews with the real counterparts. The interviews were sociological and covered factual ground about their situations, while exploring political theories and social issues. I included photos, much as Sebald later did. The narration asked the reader to find a balance between imagination and the reality of everyday life and to examine the boundaries of fiction and nonfiction. The space had been opened up in American letters by Truman Capote's *In Cold Blood*. Boundaries. Defining them gripped my mind: how to tell a story without making it up.

I felt most comfortable, though, and still do, writing poetry. It has always drawn from a larger and more mysterious source. In the Rome years, in my poems, I was close (nearly one) with words that were imminent presences—"the way yellow is inside a lemon, black inside an ant." Often my subject was unrequited love. Like

Catullus, who wrote for years about his struggle to be released from a passion for a lover who was unfaithful ("I hate and I love. Why—how—can that be, perhaps you will ask me / That I know not."), the subject of a troubled relationship and its confusing misery was the one that I, too, explored in a factual way. "There is no word for rain but rain. / There is no word at all for pain." Adrienne Rich, Sharon Olds, Louise Glück—those silence breakers would become sources once I returned to the United States, where I began using libraries again. In Rome, access to English books was rare, except through friends.

The novel remains unpublished, although an agent flew out to meet me in San Francisco after I returned to the States. He insisted that I make the heroine positive, lift her into resolution. "You can easily do it," he said. "The book is brilliant."

If I could have claimed my protagonist's fatalism as my own, I might well have changed the book's ending and, perhaps, my life. But I was unable to abandon the cry of noble defeat that issued from my female character of the late sixties. Then, it seemed a compliment that the agent should compare me to Jean-Paul Sartre. Now, it makes me laugh. "You have written *Nausea* in a female voice," he pronounced with some satisfaction. I wonder if he ever imagined where that attitude had come from.

7

The experience of Rome eventually did bring me back, not to it, not to the Tiber, but to Italy and a second marriage, this one to an Italian with green eyes and a disarmingly warm laugh. In moving back to Italy, I faced integrating an identity all over again. I experienced wholeness, as much as that can exist. The daily path has slowly created a sturdy state of mind that accepts flaws, inconsistencies, and bursts of crazy enthusiasm. The state of mind took me beyond country into a place I had sheltered from my earliest years. A self that had been wrapped, vital and censored, was free to speak.

8

When I left the courtyard, I was saddened to leave a way of life, but I was also eager to get on with things and to live in my own country again. The Tiber, of course, didn't stop talking even as I was packing. It said, Choose to exist. Flow, change. Make no mistake: You will not find what you had before. The ruins in Rome drily stated much the same thing: Loss and collapse, they happen. Passion won't be stitched together by will.

Water in Rome has always been the teacher, making bearable what is otherwise arid and heavy. The humblest municipal faucet, with its open arc dropping into the drain with SPQR below it, dribbles and always says the same thing. Go ahead, get your face wet. Bend down, yes, right on the street, and wash your hands and face and put your lips to the thin stream for refreshment. It's hot. Streets are deserted and almost causing angst. Let the flowing water cool your brow.

Except when it was under scaffolding, making Bernini's dramatic fountain look like a plaster cast, the Four Rivers, two minutes from the courtyard, cascaded and gushed with plenty. When the wind picked up, water slapped out in wet ropes. Water in Rome tempers the meaning of death. It makes waste look unimportant when compared to the sparkling power of beauty. That was the hope I carried with me when I left the courtyard.

XIX

Caravaggio

His work gave a new meaning to darkness and, by comparison, light.

1

Caravaggio, who once lived and worked on the streets between Piazza Navona and Piazza San Luigi dei Francesi, quite near the courtyard, was known as a violent man. Most likely, he fled to Rome as a twenty-year-old because of a murder he had committed in Milan. He was in endless legal battles while he lived in the Eternal City. He fled Rome, his protectors having engineered his escape, after killing another man in a sword fight.

In the nearby churches of Santa Maria del Popolo, San Luigi dei Francesi, and Sant'Agostino, his work was easily visited on daily walks. The paintings were cornerstones in my impression that living in Rome was a free dialogue among religion, interpretations of society, and the shiver of culture. The shiver was exhilarating and close to a dream. It was so easy to enter, to rest, to learn, to return.

The two paintings in Santa Maria del Popolo, *The Crucifixion of St. Peter* and *The Conversion of St. Paul on the Way to Damascus*, although commissioned by the Church, had both been troubled by criticism and rejections. Caravaggio's *Madonna di Loreto* in Sant'Agostino caused scandal because the Madonna was strong, erotic, and too similar to the unshod peasants who worshiped her son. This was a common fate for his work and good fortune for the shrewd nobles and cardinals who acquired his radical canvases in order to rescue the Church from the horrors of displaying them in sacred places.

Caravaggio's use of street people as models, his own considered lack of decorum, the humanity as opposed to the saintliness of his subjects, the way flesh was exposed down to the bare feet and dirty toes of holy women, made his work on religious subjects acceptable only to a sophisticated elite within the institutional hierarchy. The Church's rejection of his form of realism touched themes about superficiality and censorship that interested me then, with my rather predictable critical focus of repression and my attachment to rebellion. John Lennon, Joan Baez, Bob Dylan, and Mick Jagger were what popular culture was adding as comment on war, society, and sex. Many minor seventeenth-century Italian painters addressed these subjects as didactic warnings, staying on the literal surface of gruesome and terrifying subjects ranging from sadism to murder. They managed to escape controversy.

Caravaggio explored these subjects with penetrating sobriety and clarity, usually giving the viewer some sense of the transfixing consequences to those involved. He rarely stopped on the surface of the event, something he could easily have done, given his technical mastery and control. Because he was such an extraordinary painter, he stupefied his critics with talent that expressed the controversial and seemed to approach the heretical. He was not entertaining or titillating; he was translating a different vision of authority.

2

The dark streets in my area, devoid of the flares of store lights, had a medieval atmosphere that made it possible to imagine thieves jumping from shadows. They contrasted with the glossy, elegant, and pretentious life on the Via Veneto or the Corso. Walking in places where Caravaggio had brawled with poor people and nobles alike, I repeatedly imagined his life as I heard other voices rise in anger and conflict. His famous eruptions of temper and violence,

perhaps driven by his malarial fevers, always felt strangely important to me. Probably I didn't focus on the man as much as on the
sudden flares of life that felt as if they went back as far as his times
and yet somehow touched the darkness of the present. The intricate relationships in light, the shadows and the tenebrous shades
of light, the chiaroscuro of Mediterranean life, were heightened to
stark and dramatic contrasts. His work gave a new meaning to darkness and, by comparison, light. He was more than a witness and
less than a judge. A view of wholeness, an inclusion of all that
wasn't positive, was an element in his work that I was drawn to,
obviously like a beginner, looking for ways to broaden my understanding. Since the phenomenon of projection is very real in untrained eyes, I interpreted in a personal manner startling images
that expanded my ideas about life.

3

Caravaggio's paintings carry enough psychological material that
they do not need words to convey how precisely that long-ago
world matches ours. He is unrelenting in opening our eyes. He
removes the illusions of virtue as a prerogative of class. He does
not stop at appearances assured by money. His examinations of
violence, its gradations and effects, lead us to the depths of the
twentieth and twenty-first centuries. And he gives space to conversion, to sharp moments of consciousness, when radical change
occurs. He also explores seduction and some of its emotions and
effects.

Poverty, in the late sixties in Italy, was a reality that inspired
political attention and solutions. The approach to poverty was very
far from what I knew and had experienced, either in the United
States or in England. In spite of obvious class differences in Rome,
the rights of poor people and the need to support and integrate

them were not issues up for debate. Self-sufficiency had no universal currency as an expectation and at best was seen as an unrealistic default. The state as social guarantor was crucial to progress and progress assumed an elimination of class differences. Poor people were not a category for opprobrium or blame, but a reflection of the failure of the social and economic system to provide. This painter, risking rejection, proposed people who were poor as the strong and central models in his religious paintings. He did not make common people a caste to be shunned or pitied.

4

Caravaggio is now comfortably credited with being part of the birth of modernism. He has emerged as a rebel pioneer as penetrating as any of the northern painters who were searching to reveal more in character than the effects and expressions of social class. His experimentation often elicited more dangerous and radical consequences than did northern realism. He not only challenged prosperous merchants with unflattering or objective secular interpretations, as did Dutch and Flemish painters, but he exposed new material inside Christian messages and biblical stories. He shook the Catholic world.

Without the myth of the noble savage or the virtuous poor, he interpreted the good news of the Gospel as equality itself. Besides his choice of subjects, his elimination of background (think of Leonardo's wandering paths and background scenes or earlier paintings like Fra Angelico's, in which the villages rise in little geometric cones), the meandering dimension that lent an illusion of order, rationality, and place to a canvas, is removed. His sharp focus on the moment, on the person, and on penetrating light as a mediator of truth and emotion takes all stories out of an old collectivity and places them in frames where the individual is at once powerful and powerless, independent of institutions or society. This close interpretation, especially of subjects that were not single portraits, suggested elements in an individual's actions and choices that depended on moments of free choice, even in religious events. His ability to create this focus opened up perceptions of significant interior passages in human character anywhere, but especially in the Catholic world of France and Spain, where the Church was struggling to maintain its authoritarian power.

5

I used to walk the Via della Scrofa and remind myself that Caravaggio had walked the same street. It was where I had stayed in the fleabag hotel for those first days, and the basilica of Sant' Agostino was nearby. As I think of it now and search for analogies, I am curious as to why it still feels so important. The intensity of Caravaggio's work, even if it was not completely natural (and certainly not natural to me), contained elements of how I wished to write. Forgive the comparison (I was young) and accept my acknowledgment of the absurd gulf in talent and temperament. I think the attraction centers on the power he called upon to show the dark and light within a human being. Certainly, at the time I lived in Rome, the controlled ways in which women approached the full range of human behavior in literature and often in life were still restrictive. Caravaggio enveloped the contrasts and contradictions of a world supposedly guided by religion and showed the energies and passions driving it. It was a dangerous world and the messages were equally dangerous, if one was to live a Christian life without intellectual reservations. For me, he was a deep shadow figure, presenting a contrast to the thin, arrogant, and comfortable middle-class view of Anglo-Saxon life.

Yet there were other elements. One was a keen sense of obligation. My shoes, or, more accurately, sandals, which probably should have belonged to a painter had I not ceased to try because of my father's intrusions into my work, nevertheless walked on those stones knowing that my father, who had died suddenly— laughing while watching TV—had never been to Europe. Afraid of flying, he had studied art, won prizes. He had put it all away, opted for a comfortable life of responsibility once he had a family to support. After that, never a sketch, a used brush. Never museum visits for himself or with his children. I walked those streets in Rome, wearing those killing, silent shoes.

Partly certain that I did not want to die because of that same sense of denial and frustration, partly trying to understand how it was he could have put his passion away inside, I journeyed with him in my mind. What would he have thought of Caravaggio and those dark churches? I don't really know. Outside of the University Club of Milwaukee, I have few memories of being in places with him. The year before he died was the only time I ever stood in front of a painting with him. In, literally, a once-in-a-lifetime event, he suddenly bloomed and asked me to drive with him to Chicago to see an exhibit of Van Gogh's work. He said more than once, as we chatted about the thick impasto of the paint, "I never realized you could understand."

But those shoes partly worn in his name fit me well as my own. Seeing work where it had been generated was a dream. Any day, I could enter the Contarelli Chapel and stand for as long as I wished in front of the scene where Christ mysteriously invites Matthew to become a disciple. The experience was free and the paintings had been visited in that same place for four hundred years, in weather that on many days must have been similar to what I experienced when I would leave, partially blinded, coming out of the cool darkness of the chapel into real light. Then I might go a block farther and contemplate the painter's Madonna di Loreto, a sober flesh and blood woman whose baby, wrapped in white cloth and deep shadows, leaned over her arm and blessed two poor souls. Her elongated neck was as erotic and

memorable as Nefertiti's. And by then, I would nearly be bursting with the sensation of my good fortune to be in such proximity to immanence.

6

Because of his elimination of landscape, common people in Caravaggio's work were no longer shown to be of relative importance. The famous little people, the salt of the earth in Protestant sermons, were canceled in his paintings. They were not the rubes found in Hogarth or the sentimental characters in Dickens. They had none of the certainties of rank defined by costumes or role. Caravaggio found subjects in human nature, rather than in social class. In his choice of models, in his representations of cruelty and violence, physical beauty and love, he was as scrupulous with truth as he was careless of rules in his life. In the deep contrasts in light, the naturalness of his subjects intensified. These dramatic measures for character took place without the mediation of priests that the Church insisted upon. His revelations supported a radical reading of morality. Drawn to this zone of narration in his work,

I see the midwestern girl, not knowing from where to where her knowledge of the world was bridged and yet feeling she was literally touching a missing part of it in the world he portrayed. The implicit energy of violence must have also caught my unconscious side.

XX

Communism

"What are you selling?"
"Do you know the Communist newspaper *Unità*?"
  —conversation with a young man ringing the author's doorbell, 2010

1

In the late sixties, the fascination of living in a country where social equality was discussed in politics as well as in public philosophical debates was immense. It didn't take long to discover that communism was not just intellectual theory about workers or leveling wages. It was a system of belief that many members in Parliament and local governments applied to make those ideas real. The extension of benefits in education, health, housing, and progressive taxation then and now often is based on indexes that favor income redistribution: democracy as a social pact. This has many tangible and positive effects. It makes the average person feel secure. Italians will often say that knowing everyone has health care lets them sleep at night. Health care, pensions, minimal university tuition—categories of social benefits—while subject to great abuses, are seen as necessities, which, at least in part, equalize chances for all. The price of bread, *pane comune*, is still closely monitored by the government.

Marxism, because of the strength and vitality of the Italian Communist Party, was an applied political ideology; it went well beyond the naïve lip service that I paid to its more inspiring analyses about eliminating competition when I exchanged ideas, for example, with students when I was in Oxford. In England, Marxism was a real debate, far more open than in the United States. Nevertheless, it remained an abstraction, a mix of literary theory and analyses of Nigerian or Bulgarian five-year economic plans. We followed these discussions in good faith, not seeing ourselves as unqualified to propose such rigid, centralized systems for the developing world. We followed and volunteered precisely because inequality in the world seemed an injustice that fell within our generation's concerns. As we considered solutions for our own lives, this broader view never completely vanished from our reasoning.

2

Belief in communism in the late sixties in Italy, which had been given a human face by Pasolini and Gramsci, was widespread and contrasted not just in words to similar ideologies in the United States. Unlike U.S. Marxists, who held ideas that had little chance of ever being applied in their own country, those in Italy had the physical numbers, especially in the regions of Emilia Romagna, Tuscany, and Umbria, to write the concepts into law, often governing socially advanced cities. In Italy, perhaps because much of their thinking was considered virtuous and was often extremely innovative, it felt like a revolution, lived so seriously that language might even invoke violence when laying out the permanent design.

Many Italians did not blink an eye at the idea that everyone's wages, from those of workers to those of professors, should be leveled. Even today, when income tax returns of ordinary citizens are published by local governments on the Web, few people seem to raise the objection of privacy. Why not publish them, and catch rich evading devils? If you have nothing to hide, why worry if people know what your income is? Terrorism was a disturbing coda to that impressive set of plans and reforms and it complicated the issue of how change was to be brought about. The changes taken individually were easy enough to endorse when they espoused full employment or decried corruption. But the ideological commitment was strong enough to reach everywhere. How the American Revolution was taught in schools (and was still being taught when my daughter attended *liceo*) was wholly ideological. It was taught as an economic war, as was the Civil War—full stop. It was the "full stop" part of communism that made it difficult for me to think that I would ever become a member.

3

The ideology of communism favored a leveling of society that surprised me, as much as I wanted to embrace the concept of social collectivity. The Italian discourse on poverty and its solutions was fascinating, and often precisely what I wished to hear, until the certainty in their voices left me out. Just as Plath and her suicide seemed extreme when linked to feminism, the amount of denial involved in much of late sixties and early seventies orthodox leftist thinking, including its ambivalent position on violence and censorship, made me realize that I would not fit the cause, which sometimes still organized in cells. Party membership took 10 percent of one's wages, and defined life largely in material terms. Loyalty to a group that offered official positions and interpretations, and involved altering what one knew and had to deny, brought about many disturbing distortions. Ideology, at a certain point, demands a repression of views that contrast with it, even in one's own mind.

In politics in the late sixties in Italy, I was generally out of my element, although I considered myself as part of what was known as the Left. I cared too much for my own ways of thought, for freeing the broken parts in people and life, not just by social pact but also through psychological analysis and even prayer. I stood with Keats, lingering in light, in silence, in detail that reflected on uncertainty, unknowing, search. How could one deny the harsh realities of the extermination camps in Communist Russia and on the other hand force people to refute religion?

The ideological turn of mind in Communists I knew in Rome had steely qualities of certainty. Even ideological atheists were different from other atheists, it seemed to me, if they had the ideology of communism to substitute for faith. Today, because of the steadiness of Italian life and assumptions, the ideas inherent in communism persist, as does nostalgia for its eventual return or its application in some utopian form. But its general momentum and direction seem to have come to a standstill. When I lived in Rome, my tendencies roughly corresponded to the positions of a center-left party called the Partito Repubblicano, led by a decent and rigorous professor who had a shape not unlike Alfred Hitchcock's. Surveying the Europe inside the European Union, I probably am a social democrat today.

XXI

More Caravaggio

More importantly, are they gone, the old familiar faces?
In time living on into a new share of English promise, some of
the junior ones went over the wall, and that was the last we saw of *them.*

— John Ashbery, *Flow Chart*

1

It was easy to pick out Caravaggio's characters in the Campo de' Fiori, faces of his mistresses, his child, faces of those who were to become Magdalene, Saul, and Peter. Among all the other artists who surely walked the streets of Rome, from Raffaello to Bernini, I never felt that same vital shock of presence. Out of curiosity, I tried to better understand what his hold was by trying out an analogy.

The poet John Ashbery invited me once to his New York apartment. We had met when reading at the same poetry festival in Holland. He was to receive a large prize in Italy and wanted to chat about it and also, perhaps as a pretext, ask me what would be appropriate attire. During the time I was in his West Side apartment, I saw his study, met an assistant who was working at a computer, and watched him be photographed for a Swedish magazine. The photographer seemed like a character from Antonioni's *Blow-Up*. He had Mr. Ashbery sit and tilt his head, profile, front, other side, while he turned his camera and twisted his body and shifted planes, up and down, clicking away for dozens of shots. He stopped for a few seconds to reload the arsenal and then resumed the same inhuman inspection. A signature for the release and he was gone, having spoken almost no nonessential words.

If I compare my feeling that my feet were walking the same streets as Caravaggio did with my memory of meeting John Ashbery, a major writer, who is radical in his way, iconoclastic in his poetic contribution, and part of a mythical city well known to me, I do discover a few things. Of course, the comparison may be flawed in conception, a painter and a poet, one riveted by consequence and the other allied to what is almost without linkages or rational points. Yet there is something basic about culture and time to be perceived by placing these two artists in the same simple question. What do art and an artist fasten on to if not time and place?

Ashbery exists as a literary giant, challenging influence in modern letters. The spread in a Swedish magazine is one brief example of unending testimonials to the importance of his art's rich and inconclusive content. Yet who can truly identify him with a specific place? There is only a sense of time passing and noted, moments shared in elevators, in skyscrapers, in air-conditioned stores, in subways, where all rush through the same doors.

2

Differences emerge naturally from the works. What follows is what I saw in Caravaggio's paintings with my untrained eyes. My insights are not precisely those of postmodern criticism, finding new ways to read realities that were suppressed. Certainly, though, they reveal my mind at the time. I am retracing those perceptions not to show my lack of training but because I think that they are worth pointing out as part of the complex psychology that Caravaggio transferred to his work. My ideas diverge from the historical interpretations made from facts, where a painting like *David with the Head of Goliath* has been seen as Caravaggio's plea to have his own death sentence lifted. A bit cynical, a bit too certain, I think, that. It lets the viewer off the hook and lets her or him swerve out, without considering the heavier implications of Caravaggio's work.

For me, then and now, his version of David and Goliath in the Villa Borghese is a radical revelation. Instead of the long, thoughtful gaze into space portrayed in Michelangelo's *David*, where the artist lets us contemplate the intelligence and beauty of the young man and, by extrapolation, the size of the giant, the young face in Caravaggio's painting reveals sober horror, a deforming resignation to the loss of innocence. As if the guilt that the act of murder brings about presses on his whole brain, until his eyes cannot look away, David's gaze is directed at the severed head. The severed head of the terrible giant is supposedly Caravaggio's own image. But who is David, then?

The painting in the Villa Borghese was the last in a series he did on this subject. There is nothing exhilarating in David's victory. By refuting the usual triumphal vision of David, the underdog who fulfills his duty, the painter shows us experience that surely many soldiers know. He uncovers the ambivalence of taking any life, a subject Caravaggio approaches many times, including in versions of Judith killing Holefernes, and Salome receiving John the Baptist's head.

I am somewhat surprised even today by how these violent portraits and the ideas in them fascinated me. The psychology of the severed head, the illumination of the victim status of the

perpetrator of the deed must have caught my unconscious sense of my own splits and sense of guilt. I was cut off from my body and I seem to have been fumbling toward wanting to integrate what was hidden.

I liked the equality and transparency of Caravaggio's violent images. I liked the reversal. Caravaggio draws from a collective story an interpretation that most of us would like to deny. Even when murder is necessary, it marks the perpetrator. The atmosphere is complex. There is between the two figures of David and Goliath even the psychological issue of self-murder. The reckoning and lingering fallout that arise from violent actions have been foregrounded. That nightmarish perception is censored often, even today.

3

Ashbery's work offers litanies of words and the flowchart of a world lost to shared meaning. It is filled with runs of inconsequentiality, luxury, and excess that cannot be staunched or judged. He sings his own song and we cannot quite get the words. He cannot abandon a sentimental nostalgia for the surplus and the lightness that come with an inability to feel guilt, or the importance of guilt, because the basis for that guilt cannot be sorted out.

Ashbery finds language that mocks and records the way the Western world goes ahead, unchecked, generating data and information but unable to contain it long enough to define cause and effect. In the timidity of relationships and in their mystery, in the noise and ways truths are deflected with less effort than it would take to shoo away a fly, he writes poems that are designed to be barely comprehensible, in spite of their fascinating density. They are words set free from centuries of pattern and connotation and captured by an individualistic transcription.

Caravaggio paints, without rhetoric or sentimentality, truths

that few of us wish to see. He does not let us slip away. His exciting images flicker back and forth between things and what we
know about those things. In *The Conversion of St. Paul*, in the
angle Caravaggio chooses, so that the man tips nearly out of the
frame headfirst into our laps, the momentum is so emphatic that
we feel we should get out of the way or be knocked down by his
physical presence. Saul's upended position suggests birth and its
violent helplessness. Saul's passage to becoming Paul means turning upside down. In those little Roman streets, in my life in the
courtyard, I felt the first connections between place and action in
my own sallies toward discovering a life.

Caravaggio leaves searing marks in the memory of Rome,
with its tolerant and overblown acceptance and its dark periods of
repression. Partly because we can visit Caravaggio and revisit him,
stand right in front of Saint Matthew's flaying for as long as we
need to and then turn to the other wall, where Christ is first inviting Matthew to become a disciple, access to his work is so easy
that he becomes nearly a synonym for the close relationship of

life to art. Caravaggio draws us in, showing depths that make us squirm when we recognize that his characters could reside in ourselves. In the Contarelli Chapel, his own frightened and disturbed portrait in the back row of the crowd watching Saint Matthew being flayed is an offering like a mirror. Conflict can turn reality almost completely on its head. If we fail to react and only passively witness evil, while failing to speak about its existence, truth is lost. The midwestern girl suffered without knowing why when she saw his stricken face. Yet his clarity in bringing out the psychological dimension of realism made the existence of meaning and the possibility to define it almost obvious.

4

Ashbery, instead, creates continuity that is static. While amusing, his words weigh one down with anxiety. His language webs, however they may shine in light, do not attach to New York City in such ways that they remain clearly identifiable with the skyscrapers, or the rivers, or the masses of people moving on the sidewalks. Ashbery's modernity, which seems and is new, and certainly not abstract, will never find a context in Italy to give his flow the space to do more than form an individual transcription of a state of mind. His riff is a world of its own. The past is not history to be searched for larger patterns. However he fills the page and takes us in, we are fundamentally cut loose, without context, without community.

5

In the neighborhood trattoria where I often was served a second glass of wine by a waiter named Pasquale, I knew that the statue of Giordano Bruno, erected on the spot where he was burned in

1600, was only two minutes away. I knew that I would pass it on my path back to the courtyard. His hooded face, when I saw it, was vaguely reminiscent of Lincoln's in the Lincoln Memorial, except that Giordano Bruno died right there, burned like the Salem witches. The market stalls, the barking dogs, the flower stands, and cinema Essai, where all of Gian Maria Volonté's films, or Pier Paolo Pasolini's, or Lina Wertmüller's, could then be seen for three hundred lire a showing, could not lessen the immediacy of Bruno's tragedy or his resistance.

Bruno was burned for his observations about the universe's unpredictability. Under the bronze cowl of the monk's hood, his head is bent in admonishment. The brooding monument forced the market sweepers to detour around it. The scraping of the stick brooms sounded not like *Tsk-tsk* but *The world is so much larger than you*. The world, even in the face of all this beauty, can be terrifying and unjust. Terror and injustice not only counterweight beauty; they will continue to define life. And yet, so will beauty. This light, this radiance, blinding, dancing, like love, rushes to fill us with wonder.

XXII

Repetition

There is an inviolable in loco parentis, the past itself in its messy forms.

1

Even now that Rome's souvenir stands are run by Indians, and the Campo de' Fiore itself is full of ahistorical Irish pubs, the restaurant in which I had that Frascati wine still pays the same Pasquale I knew when he and I were without graying hair, and without much of the experience that has likely made each of us redefine our sense of what is important beyond earning a decent wage or raising a family. There is seldom, even after years of absence, a feeling of absolute change in Rome. Things might be dingier or things might have been cleaned up. The city coffers might be brimming or horrifyingly empty. But most things will still be recognizable.

This is continuity: not only the huge Renaissance Cancelleria, a block away, which obviously can't move, but seeing the same faces in a place where the napkins are still cloth and the orders of cannelloni served in forty years must add up to a fairly daunting stack of dishes. This stability, which is sniffed by tourists but never understood in all its implications, its weight, its repetition, fits the repetitions of the Mass, the ecclesiastical calendar, the customs that make an *amatriciana* a Roman dish and *tortelli di erbette* a dish from the north.

This adherence to repetition, to proven and good things or, perhaps, not even good but known, gives a security to anyone who visits Italy. In spite of all the fussing about inefficiency or backwardness, it is precisely this immovability that, like morning light, asserts that change has limits and is cyclical. This repetition and richness is the opposite of Ashbery's versions of stasis and heavy fare. The word *repetition*, which generates boredom and alienation in Ashbery, has positive connotations in Italy, where it lends stability to every day and calls for elaborating rituals in order to keep life moving and interesting at the same time.

This quality, which promotes or, at least, tolerates lapses in order to assure that all that is good remains, too (saving the baby instead of throwing out the bathwater), rescues many of us, slows us down, and, in that suspended state of thrashing and turning, finally lets us come to accept what we have, thus keeping us from despair. In Italy, at the end of the day, someone lights the stove and prepares with some attention a meal to break the rhythm or boredom. It is impossible not to feel that the world is enough or at least offers some compensation when a bowl of spaghetti, with olive oil and two fresh tomatoes and a sprig of basil, appears once again. In that simplicity and commitment, the sense of repetition has a meaning.

2

In Italy, the tangled and mysterious strata of those who lived before surrounds, consoles, horrifies, surprises, suffocates. But it never concludes that mere diversion is the end. We count on the Italian reservoir of responses and solutions as we search for our own private sense of the whole. Here, in spite of the modern Italian state that allows divorce and abortion and so much else that is considered part of the secular state, there is an inviolable in loco parentis, the past itself in its messy forms, which will not allow us to define ourselves as unshepherded beings operating in unfiltered, unprocessed, unprecedented reality. There is no such thing. We are always accompanied by ancestors. We never are wholly alone or original. We will never escape evil or contradiction or hold absolute knowledge. The past in Italy, even when it proposes nihilism or absurdity, will not let that single voice stand. Stephen Hawking will explain why there is no God, and before he can complete his argument, there will be a countervoice, a counter-proof, filling the silence with a view of time that is larger than his conception.

Ashbery is most of us. He represents himself, a modern with a modern and modest context of fragments and not the whole of anything. His relationship to the city of New York is centered on himself and his own perception, and that simply does not extend the metaphors or profound concerns that make Caravaggio, whose work has lived for four centuries in situ, such a strong and con-trastingly suitable partner for Rome and its realities of permanent chiaroscuro.

Caravaggio shows us the labyrinth that leads us to a sense of what and who we are. He gives meaning to struggle, to the city where all classes mingle, not in a rational context, but within his definition of an absolute sense of self and time. He opens views of the human heart and does not flinch in front of evil and the ele-ments strong enough to resist it. His originality rises above that of so many other artists because he manages to interpret the time-less human condition as energy, revealing, in darkness, fires of all kinds.

Ashbery, opaquely tentative, murmurs about the absurdity of adding things up into a meaningful story. In an eternal present, the flow goes on its merry, ironic, and inconsequential way, picking up from insult and injury and moving forward, past junk and de-bris, in the frame of a single life and modernity. He records babble that could be anywhere. Without the realism of place to remind us of how our lives are organized and supported, he creates expe-rience that seems to be operating without gravity and its laws. It is only in that world that nothing has real weight.

XXIII

60 Percent

Italy possesses 60 percent of all the world's works of art. Maintaining them is an impossible task.

1

One more memory pushed through the door that opened with Antonella's screams: Bernini's statue of Apollo and Daphne that rests in the Villa Borghese. When I first visited it in the sixties, it was dingy.

The joy and frustration of being loaded with as much treasure as Italy possesses often means that what you hoped to find is under repair. The maintenance of 60 percent of all the world's works of art is both an impossible task and a direct consequence of holding art as an essential reflection of society. Once repair is undertaken, a work can disappear for years, leaving in its place only an inventory number on a catalog card thumbtacked to a wall, with silk wallpaper faded around the space where the painting was.

I recently revisited the cleaned Daphne and Apollo statue, whose restoration had been corporately sponsored. The fact that the Villa Borghese was closed for years and when it reopened was nearly identical, albeit more sparkling in appearance, to what it had been was a stunning demonstration of the philosophy of stopping time, allowing for few revisions. In this beautifully ordered dwelling, the slightly dry creak from the floors and heavy curtains held a promise: Your memories will not be subjected to the violence of innovation. Here death and loss have been tactfully suspended. Spotless now, and well lit, the gracious rooms give the feeling of visiting a great noble who miraculously has managed to hang on to her fortune. Many of the most famous statues, like Bernini's *David*, have been settled in a specific room since the time they were commissioned by Cardinal Scipione Borghese centuries ago.

2

Italy makes some bold and exciting moves in modern architecture, but often prevailing wisdom remains conservative. Why change a good thing? That thinking can mean that even an opera house like the Fenice in Venice, which has burned down twice, will still be rebuilt as a copy of the copy. It means, too, that when a new statement is called for, like the Rome railroad terminal elegantly modified and rebuilt by Montuori and Vitellozzi to signify progress and the end of a terrible war, it is usually approved once it has been established how it builds on architectural precedents. Like a phoenix, it then promises rebirth.

Renzo Piano has set up a studio once again in Italy, but his desire to smash molds led him first to London and France, where he was free to enlarge a vocabulary that confronted tradition. The Italian architect Paolo Portoghesi has eased in a commanding mosque in Rome by harking back to the time of the early Renaissance. In the designs for the modern mosque and the one he has projected for Florence, he strikes architectural notes familiar from when Islam and Christianity acknowledged each other's power more than one thousand years ago.

3

In the sculpture of the myth of Daphne and Apollo, Bernini portrays Daphne at the moment in which, in order to escape being raped, she is becoming a laurel tree. Bernini, whose *David* is in the same museum—a David whose clamped mouth and crouching position make him look like a javelin thrower aiming for a world record—offers the story of Daphne in a beautiful four-sided perspective that expresses different processes in the moment of transformation. Her marble toes are turning into thin marble roots. Apollo's fingers pressed into her belly are not brutal because the escape, her transformation, is under way. From the other side, we see her hair obscuring her face. The locks are rising into branches and leaves. This point in narration, the moment in which all her energy is compacted into her hair, is transfixing. Her face from this angle is obscured. Her head, too, is obscured by the energy; her hair is part flame and part leafy branches that will defend her soul from a sexual assault. To save her identity, she is going to live as another kind of being, in another body, in another kind of memory and experience. Her mouth seen from the front is open and slightly twisted in a scream. When I recently saw the statue in its glowing clean form, I could not take my eyes off of Daphne, especially from the side where her head is disappearing. The silence she was about to enter overwhelmed me. I wanted to rush toward her.

4

Bernini's depiction quiets the violence of a rape that is interrupted. He softens the story and moves into enchantment. The sculptor has shown such virtuosity that it is hard not to marvel. As is true in great art, the incredible energy in the work can withstand my as well as others' projections.

Many critics have read into the representation the fact that Cardinal Scipione Borghese, who commissioned it, was rumored to be a homosexual. Some have suggested that the statue was a gift to him, depicting a psychological struggle: male and female in one body, enduring unconsummated pain, passion, and interruption.

Perhaps that would explain the lack of consequence. Not only was it depicting a myth; it was showing symbolically the elements in one psyche.

But I followed the myth. The story was about a woman who loses her human life and becomes a wooden form. I identified with each strand of hair that was neutralized and turned into botanical life. Her destiny was interrupted by boyish Apollo's lust. I was swept up by the energy Bernini releases, the fascinating process, but then I was horrified by its final impact. The action was gorgeous.

At some level, the hermaphrodite theory works for the statue, because Bernini seems to be far more caught up in the beauty of perfection than in the emotion generated by Daphne's fate. The subject, had it been rendered by Caravaggio, would not have looked away from darker effects: the impact of Apollo's action for himself as well as the psychological sacrifice of transformation for Daphne. Duccio, who had portrayed the Madonna with her inner gaze fixed on all that life brings, including trials of suffering and sorrow, would have been better able to represent the reality of Daphne and Apollo, because he would not have found its embodiment in a representation of action.

Bernini's elegant skill draws attention to the fascination of metamorphosis and loses, in the excitement, the perplexing and profound tragedy, not just of the struggle but also of the sacrifice of the young female's life. Yet there is no doubt that besides its stunning beauty, the interpretation—the superficiality of Apollo's lust, his unawareness, the nearly Arcadian elements in the chase—makes it a tale that stimulates thought, that deflects rather than confronts the tragedy in the myth.

Another of Bernini's statues in the same museum, the abduction of the wildly resisting Proserpina, misses the chime of consequence as Bernini proposes excitement and drama as ends in themselves. Dynamic frenzy and struggle are the messages. The identification with the female victims has been smoothed over; all that remains is a mesmerizing effect. By enveloping such archetypal stories, and expressing attitudes of the times, these two sculptures reach through to us and unlock feelings in today's world. We meet them in the restored rooms, still caught on their marble pedestals.

XXIV

Forests and Trees

It's the winds that twitter like flutes and sometimes merge into oboes, clarinets, and horns.

1

Once my husband began to do genetic research on forests, trees, and tiny water organisms, breakfast conversations often became lively reports of discoveries. So much detail made mornings exciting. Sometimes it could be an incidence of cannibalism in a creature much smaller than a raindrop that had previously been reported to be disinterested in consuming its own kind. Sometimes the results of the activity of genetic lines of beech showed far more complexity than had been imagined. There was a moment when we planned to visit all the old or ancient trees in Italy, photograph them, and write a book that suggested itineraries through villages that honored the arboreal veterans. We would catalog trussed beech trees and olive trees on crutches, testifying to mysteriously long lives in out-of-the-way places. Environmental survival and change seemed angles that would interest tourists.

My husband planned to include maps of land-reclamation projects and interventions necessitated by cataclysmic natural events, starting from Roman times. The history of man's impact, destructive and reparatory, makes Italy an intricate land puzzle, touched and retouched like a patient who has never stopped having surgery, or a painting that has undergone restorations in nearly every century. He wanted to develop brief tourist trips along artificially constructed banks where rivers run above the level of the villages and eventually past reclamation projects done to eradicate malaria in swamps. It would have been a book with a unique historical focus and a series of useful social, economic X-rays about the country. Of course, local restaurants would have had their own place, as well. Then his health took a turn as abrupt as a lava spill. The plans for the book stopped as suddenly.

But in many ways, we were lucky. What is life in Italy if not a series of responses that build upon continuity and work around destructive surges, finding solutions to go ahead, knowing adaptation continues. And rather than making flailing attempts to resist change, a general position insists, Why not stay still—not moving precipitously toward anything new. The entire social system encourages and allows for this response. Why not lean on all that refuses to change? Why not admit that your job will wait for you without anyone pressuring you to return? Why assume that society does not owe you assistance through tough times? These supports may be part of finding a way out. So live with the stasis. Take your time to explore the reasons for living before rushing back into being productive. We organized our responses according to these expectations.

Even though great mistakes were made in diagnosing and finding the path to come back from the stroke, we never feared the chaotic loss of one's job or the withdrawal of medical help. That brought back so keenly my father's situation when he had his heart attack. He was fifty-one. He died on the day his company's president told him that since he had not yet recovered from a stroke that had exhausted his insurance, he was being put on half pay. Each month in my husband's recuperation brought up the blow my father had endured. Pop was a civic leader who believed in the fairness of the American system, and it was the narrowest interpretation of profit and profitability that felled this loyal and productive man. The sterile seeds planted in his story came back in our struggle and slowly sprouted with hope, at last.

2

Besides conferring their beauty on us and marking the seasons with gashes and gushes of excess—pollen, changing palettes of colors and shedding leaves—there are many other ways trees touch our existences: oxygen, houses, forest fires. In the Midwest, the maple sap dripping from little spigots into pails was part of a magical childhood legend, as were the sheets of bark I peeled from birches and glued to balsa models of Indian canoes. Putting my arms around a fraction of the trunk of an oak was a gesture of affection in childhood. Then one day, as a grown-up, in a park near our home, its bark against my cheek felt like the tenacious solidity I needed. While I clung to it, embarrassing tears, spontaneous, cleansing, rushed along, offering relief as I leaned on its impassive strength.

3

Italy was deforested by the Romans because of relentless demand for wood for the empire's expansion and wars. Forests provided all the fuel for smelting and mining, heating, cooking, for building supports and roofs in homes, ships, military vessels. The mind-set is all too familiar to us moderns, since the destruction of forests has continued many of the same trends the world over, including clearing land in order to exploit it for purposes of agriculture or construction. The one-sided thinking that brings about deforestation is as immediate and self-centered now as when Cicero said that "all things in this world which men employ have been created and provided for the sake of men."

Having destroyed its forests in Roman times, Italy has attempted to rebuild forests, rethink forests, manage forests, developing philosophies not only about their maintenance but on how to refashion their identity, replenishing them with nonnative trees. Planting ahistorical forests touches off fierce and bitter debates in regional discussions. Italy has a terrible history with woods and fire, including the nearly annual August blazes that are set by criminals and burn through carefully nurtured areas. Their flames scream across the nightly news, while buckets of water dangling from helicopters or light planes dump what seem to be ineffectively thin streams into roiling red explosions.

4

Forests were another language that I had scant knowledge of before living in Italy. There is a historical language about trees and a biological one. I followed the biological story of a study done over time on a patch of red spruce in the Dolomites, as my husband recounted it over many, many breakfasts. If the writer in me tells the scientific tale in factual terms, the facts by themselves will release a feeling of the poetry science inspires.

Samples were taken from the trees. The idea was to establish kinships, and understand parentage within the patch. It was assumed that the trees, given the density of the stand and its isolation from other spruce populations, had formed relationships

among themselves, like people in small villages who were forced by geographical limits into a form of inbreeding.

Each tree was labeled and each had its DNA identified. The result revealed that most of the trees were pollinated by spruce not found in the stand. There was a dominant tree among those being tested, but most received their chance to be perpetuated from trees that were nowhere within sight. The pollen grains, from faraway places, whirred in on birds' wings, insects, and on winds. In my mind, these latter elements form a permanent orchestra that enriched these isolated lives. The birds warble. The insects rasp and hum. It's the winds that twitter like flutes and sometimes merge into oboes, clarinets, and horns. Together, all move back and forth, going deeply across the trees' branches, renewing them.

5

The quietly intriguing story of these trees was recorded through the monklike activity of measuring, in different seasons, in different years. Basic observations, systematically collected like those made by the monk Mendel, who first noted the laws of genetic inheritance in the simple patterns of peas, illuminate activity that otherwise confounds appearances. There is not a day when Italian newspapers do not recount histories of scientific discoveries and debates. Often they reveal a note of national pride and a touch of resentment at the fact that Italy has been stereotyped as not worthy of serious consideration. Today in the science section, the headline features Vincenzo Tiberio, who in 1895, well before the English, published a paper on "the extracts of molds." PENICILLIN, the headline reads, AN ITALIAN DISCOVERY.

Italians have made historically significant discoveries in various scientific fields, and almost all Italy's current scientists have their origins in the public educational system. Roughly 90 percent of the school-age population attends public institutions. A Swiss professor of biochemistry at one of America's best universities said that Italian graduate students were superior to any other group: They were hardworking, had excellent theoretical backgrounds, and were generally overly modest.

Vincenzo Tiberio's present-day relatives report that he harbored no bitterness for not having been credited with part of the discovery, much less awarded a Nobel Prize. He explained his position long ago: "Love," he said. "I did science for love."

6

Newspapers and television series feature centuries of science, often revisiting centenaries of births and deaths: Galileo, Marconi, Madame Curie, Lucretius, Darwin. These are explorers to be credited with changing society as much as are rapacious conquerors taking lands for kings, or religious hordes fighting infidels.

Science lives, for all the lamentation about lack of research in Italy, and it percolates in a way that is different from the way it does in Anglo-Saxon cultures. It is not seen as something apart from culture, from the humanities. Science, the systematic identification of characteristics and mechanisms in the physical world, is as deep a part of Italian identity as wine or walking. Knowledge leads back to a single root found in language and logic. It is sometimes shadowed and its results censored or deformed by the long-standing religious authority of the Catholic Church, but the tradition of science extends to the ancients and certainly was carried forward and kept alive, as well as challenged, by the Church itself.

Science appears in daily newspapers as well as at school and on prime-time television. The story of evolution, for example, is not under fire in Italy as a subject perhaps unsuitable to be taught in public schools. Many truths held by the secular state are defended and allowed by the Church to be promulgated in what they call "their proper sphere." Stem-cell research is an example where the state gives funding, in spite of heated debates.

Yet when the issue of fertilizing embryos outside of the womb was to be voted on in a national referendum, the Pope spoke to Catholics in televised sermons, telling them to abstain from voting, because the knowledge needed to understand the issue, he said, was too complex for them to consider having an opinion. The referendum failed to reach a quorum precisely because voters were influenced by the Church's, in my opinion, inappropriate intervention.

XXV

Corrections

Time is touching things with one's hands and thinking, This is the good life.

1

When I edit Italian research papers, I tug here and there to put the English on track. The way sentences are cast by nonnative speakers often means they cannot be completely redirected. Sometimes I see texts several times. Sometimes then, I notice that what I removed the week before has been stubbornly restored. Like some of my own domestic efforts at reform by throwing out pairs of old pants or worn-out sheets, revision is often futile. Change is not accepted and the old sneaks back in. Trust is rarely offered without skepticism, and many people have little training in letting go.

Revising papers in Rome, while I lived there, was quite easy. No one tried to challenge my thoughts. This almost fits a negative stereotype of southerners, that they are laissez-faire. Instead, I tend to interpret their attitude of acceptance as quite often representing their broader sense of other cultures and more modest self-assessments.

In the north, where the political movement for economic separatism has grown in the past fifteen years, editing scientific papers has made me think of imperial Rome in its last centuries. Then citizens resisted in a battle for identity. The virtue of self-preservation and the idea of the good soldier were blinding ideals. Locating a new sense of trust that understands common good as defined by another culture—which is what would be needed to get the English into a proper form—can still turn into a cultural battle, with the style of the paper being a spoil of war.

2

In modern Italian literary writing, repetition of nouns and verbs is a sin. Synonyms must be found and an elegant trail of twists and turns, often rather heavy and meaningless, must be made so that learning and pattern prevail over simplicity. When some of my work was being translated into Italian, the issue of repetitions immediately caused a line of resistance.

I've had the following conversation—with variations—countless times.

"Why find another word if that is the word I mean?"

"Because it doesn't sound Italian."

"Well, was repetition ever decent Italian?"

"Maybe at the time of Boccaccio. He repeated phrases and it was acceptable. But probably by the time of Bembo, in the early sixteenth century, variation was introduced. He codified Dante's Italian."

"So from the early sixteenth century until the present, are you saying that a rule against repetition guides all writers who write well in Italian?"

"More or less. Since the language was absorbing popular usage, perhaps synonyms were introduced to show that the mind was not just idling on words by copying spoken usage. Changing the word within the paragraph is a way of showing that the writer is crafting something, not just repeating thoughts in his mind. It probably was a way of signaling intensified intention, and erudition. Maybe that ensured the insertion of passages and phrases by earlier writers."

"If we use repetitions in translating my work, does that make it sound bad in Italian?"

"Yes, it makes it seem as if the translator is no good. A reader will assume that she remained literal and followed the English."

"But by eliminating simple transparency about use of repetition, doesn't style overtake meaning and leave it empty? What about the author's intention and her rhythm? Aren't they paramount to a basic voice?"

"It depends. Repetition does not lend itself to creating a more solid argument or a more authentic voice. Rather, it largely contributes to boring a reader."

3

Rome never had lots of jobs to offer. What came up was to be accepted, even if it defied logic or exceeded one's experience. A contract for copyediting a three-hundred-page book of conference proceedings on information systems seemed dubious from the start. Those were days of hand-set type, where each line had to be typed into a lead bullet and then arranged one piece after the other. Each mistake meant not only retyping the correction with the linotype machine but retyping six or seven lines in order to fit the correction into justified margins.

Of course I was young, so little seemed daunting. But the four men who typeset for me were not. They did not read or speak English, which meant that half the lines set ended in words

that spilled over and had to be split. They had no idea how or where.

It is difficult to convey the scene that went on into the night, often until two or three in the morning, with the heat and noise of banging machines, and cats wandering in and out, when the inked page appeared and half the lines came to an end with amputations that were absolutely deadly. Efforts were made, but, all in all, there was no hope for finding a system that would ensure that the junctures would be right, other than blind luck. The page would be reset, with the hope that with each revision, the errors would die down.

This repetitive torture went on for three weeks, with four men, whose hands grew dirtier and dirtier, but who never turned sour when proof after proof was rejected. They went back to the linotype and split the words again, like men wearing blindfolds. However many times I sent them back, they went.

Pride and extreme flexibility fueled their bullish obedience. With their hands black and greasy with ink and oil from the press, with the dirt smashed under nails that had been doing that hard job since adolescence, we walked the syllables to decent separations, line by line, night after steaming night, until pages had come to their perfect conclusions. Then they would respectfully offer me a warm beer from bottles they kept on a shelf.

Rosina was awake and would pop open her shutters when I returned. Certainly I never minded, at least in this instance. While housemothers in college were a reason to invent ways to crawl in windows, just to prove one's independence, her vigil was a nice touch as I walked over broken glass and past cats that were sleeping. Like the moon, her presence was a benign one. It was useless to explain that no lover was involved. It was useless to explain the skill and patience of people doing a task for which they had the wrong tools. The sheer sweat of typesetting and then the tolerance for frustration in order to do the job right gave me one more example of tenacity and patience rarely credited to Italians or

Romans. We strained and risked, working without hope of over-
time. This stamina and the ability to repeat and repeat is a quality that has ramifications that run like an underground river
through the culture. The final book was a masterpiece of Italian
craftsmanship.

4

Printers and typesetters and artisans in Italy have patience and
skill that is nearly unknown, even in Western Europe. The high
standards never cease to amaze. Hands and how Italians use them
constitute national treasures. The hands that knead bread, tailor
suits, plane the arcs of cellos, weave, throw ceramics, operate
complex robots are an integral part of national identity.

The appendages that speak as loudly as words in any conversation, the gestures and the gesticulation that appear in Italian
painting and theater, also buzz with uncommon abilities. The
wrist flips to make the foam on a cappuccino turn into the design
of a pine tree or a heart. The three calla lilies arranged among
lilacs that are instinctively shaken as if hair were being fluffed.

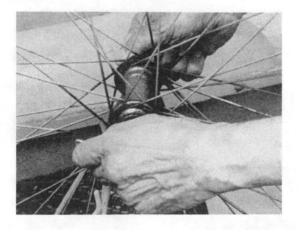

The strong and soft ways of taking hold of a body in lovemaking. The gestures of hands making, improving, correcting. The action of hand and heart, a link that I stress for students who wish to be writers—do write some parts of your text by hand; touch each word—is still seen in Italy as a good way to use one's time. Hands make every day emotionally expressive and shape sameness into surprise. In Parma, hands automatically gravitate toward perfecting, ordering, arranging. A stack of wood is never a random heap. A garden's beds always look like soft velvet pillows.

The activity of emptying the many crevices in a pinecone so that *pinoli* can be sprinkled into pesto sauce is an Italian way of spending time. The patience in fingers touching hundreds of seeds one by one links to the pleasure of place and eating together. The perception of abundance, if it is found in uses for the smallest things, can still satisfy, if time has no particular commercial meaning. Much life continues to emerge at this level: finding oregano in bushes; blackberries gleaming through thickets and thorns; playing a good hand of *briscola* slapped down in a center for old people. How much there is to look forward to when eating, especially, is seen as personal pleasure as well as communal good.

Hands and what it takes to prepare meals are guided by un-

spoken rules similar to written Italian. They transform the nouns *tomato* and *wheat*, and find synonyms so that repetition can be traced in slight alternatives. Why farfalle and rigatoni, mezze penne, and fusilli shapes, if not to repeat pasta without repeating it?

5

This quality of patience found in hands and fingers holds my attention. There is patience for chopping, and peeling, for recopying, for doing so many tasks in daily life well. The young butcher apprenticed in the local supermarket showed me his hands. "I had cuts everywhere in the first six months. The knives are sharp and I was shaky. But now I can control the blade, and choose the knife, and cut away the fat." The way he touches the meat without big machines, those violent saws hacking through bone, that learning and willingness to teach the fingers something worth learning, all this carries with it a conservative and traditional idea. His scars carry messages of improvement and the importance of correct ways. His cutlets meet a standard; while not that of the golden age exemplified by Rosina's short Roman butcher, they reflect the idea of making a cutlet that is something to be admired. He plans to be a butcher for life. Keeping hands trained, alive, touching what we use, adds to a sensation of proportion, whether it be making a beautiful sandwich by hand or working on computers, and letting go of the idea of time while one works to perfect a final proof. Here, though often the outcome of a job falls short of what one hoped, it just as often fuels passion or inspiration. If that happens, the bill remains the same, while the time spent to match the color or arrange the page may increase ten times.

Often, flexibility, inventing a solution where none exists, is agility that has been developed with an eye on tradition. Tradition confirms that there is a solution for anything to be pulled from the past. Costs have put traditional skills under pressure, but they have made few inroads into the pleasure of spending time using one's hands for fabricating things that can be shared. "Of course," my neighbor says, "I make gnocchi. There is so much more pleasure in eating them than just mashing the potatoes."

XXVI

Restoration

Neither let your motive be the fruit of action, nor let your attachment
be to non-action.

—Bhagavad Gita

1

The Benedictine order has work at its center. Manual labor is a way of knowing existence and exploring its meaning. Hands are the counterbalance to study, to prayer. They put one in touch with life. Although it never happened during the Rome years, the many versions of the Catholic Church as history, intellectual thought, mystical search filtered in and fell on me, a bit like the spruce that receives fertilization from airborne and invisible sources, and left new seeds.

There was, for example, a conversation with a Canadian who had become a monk serving in Italy and who was struggling to come to terms with a different culture and the somewhat closed dynamic of the relationships within the order. He mentioned how his work with his hands and with wood was the main reason he had been able to persevere and invest his calling with meaning. Eventually, at a retreat, which began with a climb through a forest in the Tuscan Apennines, where some of the trees remained from medieval times, I met him again.

The forest, a source of wealth and identity integral to the founding of the order, suggested wonderful photos along the way, had there been light. But the height of the trees made it difficult for me to find more than a few spaces outside of the deep shadows. The walk first to the monastery and then on to the hermitage, founded in 1012 C.E., extended the continuity of the trees' solemnity. Beech, chestnut, maples, oaks, and powerful appearances of water and waterfalls, cutting back and forth through the mountains, showed nature in relationship to its custodians.

People on Sunday outings to gather chestnuts were scattered on flatter, lower fields. Admonitions, like "wanted" posters tied to trees, announced in no uncertain terms that a permit was obligatory in order to collect them. The gathering activities were frenzied, with children darting to and fro, waving the green spiky balls protecting the nuts. People bent and scoured and tumbled out from hedges with bags so full, it made one wonder if the permits had any meaningful limits. The scene suggested some of Brueghel's paintings of children and their games.

2

This ancient Apennine forest in the Middle Ages was the economic and spiritual base of the community built above it. At that time, forests for Christians were a metaphor for the desert in the New Testament. They were an unknown, a set of wild conditions that harbored darkness that might envelop the devil, evil, and eventual death. They had an allegorical meaning to someone who was trying to find God. They were also basic resources. The work of the order involved harvesting the trees and transporting them all the way down to the sea, where the beautiful timber would be used for building. The income supported the religious order.

At the time of unification (in the 1860s), the lands ceased to belong to the order and became the property of the newly founded state of Italy. In 1929, Mussolini signed a treaty recognizing the Vatican state, and the Church was allowed to rent the buildings and sometimes the lands that had formerly been its property at nearly no cost. The forests, which are marvelously profound, are now both owned and managed by the Italian government. The presence of the monastic order remains a guarantee of their historical and metaphorical significance. The number of monks has dwindled far more drastically than the health and number of the trees.

3

Climbing up through occasional light and much shaded semi-darkness feels like walking through a series of veils. The sounds of water, the rush of winds in high branches are joined by the murmurings of people making recreational use of the forests, and then by the more muted sounds of people climbing to reach the churches at the top. In a forest so old, and so far from everyday life, the veils of light slipping through the tall trees suggest mystical feelings. In the late Middle Ages, when followers of Saint Francis and others like him were building monasteries in savagely remote and forested mountain places like La Verna and Camaldoli, echoing the experience of Saint Benedict at Subiaco and Monte Cassino, the extreme isolation was felt to be an aid to meditation.

4

The Canadian was undertaking his own search. The life of the monk was ordered by periods of prayer and those of work. Finding purpose in that life, which combined the silence of the separate cells in which each monk lived alone with communal prayer and meals, was proving difficult. The rituals did not seem sufficient for the building of genuine community and the development of a common purpose. In order to ground himself, the Canadian had begun to work on a very dilapidated unoccupied cell, which still retained its original wooden paneling; similar paneling had once lined the walls and ceilings of each monk's small cell. He cleaned and treated each plank of special pine, originally hewn from the forest, some of it as long ago as the fourteenth century. After five years, he had nearly completed the task of restructuring, cleaning, treating, and waxing the wood, making visible its large knots and pronounced marbled rings. In the center of the garden of the cell (several small, interconnected rooms), he had mounted a large stone ball he had found in a part of the hermitage complex, originally ammunition for a catapult used by the Venetians who had attacked the monastery when they had been at war with Florence. Its round white shape added to a garden that had not been weeded since the monk had turned his every spare hour to restoring the wood paneling inside.

He had scavenged for panels of antique timber to substitute

for ones that had been ruined. He roamed the attics and storage places under stairs in the monastery. His discovery of curved pieces that fitted a vaulted ceiling of the cell's oratory gave him the impetus to go on. But his work was not understood by the other brothers, who thought it unnecessarily demanding of time and effort. For him, though, the metaphor of restoration, bringing something old and decayed to new life, releasing the life, the color and perfume, of the wood, was in itself enough to delight and sustain him, representing the possibility of bringing new life to ancient institutions. Working with his hands made him humble about all that physical labor entails. The rooms and their darkish red tones came back burnished by his labor.

5

The monk who granted permission for changes was often so slow that much of the restoration had to proceed discreetly, without permission. Many guests took a lively interest in the project, among them architects, engineers, and other professionals who offered advice and gave the Canadian the products necessary for bringing the wood back to life and preserving it. In the last phase of the work, the monk was assisted by a retired master carpenter, who, moved by the task per se as well as by the monk's fervor, helped him to secretly lift an entire wall by many inches and fix it in its original position, since otherwise the structure of the room would have remained seriously compromised. This was done without permission, because approval for such a major intervention was highly problematic. It was done without the brotherly participation he had imagined.

The monk let me take pictures. The large pine knots characteristic of this ancient wood were dark and often not unlike the screaming mouth in Edvard Munch's famous painting. Since the wood lined all surfaces, the restored rooms hovered, sometimes

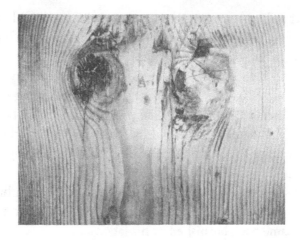

in a comforting way, sometimes oppressively. We shared his warm feeling for the wood-paneled rooms whose restoration had helped him give meaning to the loneliness of these years. He had saved something, even if it was not as significant as human souls. The wood had drunk gallons of various products and waxes and been rubbed back into a state of health. The wood contained centuries. But, unspoken, the question remained: Is this enough for a life? Are we as dry and passive as pine?

The monk had us tiptoe to a small window in one of the rooms that overlooked a private chapel built in the thirteenth century by a cardinal. We peeked down and could feel exactly how a monk who lived as a recluse in this cell could witness the celebration of Mass at the altar underneath.

The paneled rooms and the monk's sincere, unsolved search for spiritual growth brought back the position of an American monk whose book *The Seven Story Mountain* I had read when I lived in Rome. Thomas Merton documented in his extensive journals his struggles with faith and restless solitude. During the time I lived in Rome, Merton died in Bangkok when he touched a faulty fan. Ever fascinated by the Eastern way of thinking, he had followed that path east as the war in Vietnam raised many germaine questions about faith, as well as politics. Where were the conjunctions in the two? His journals in the last days of his life describe a near-mystical encounter of the two points of view, Eastern and Western—the merging of apparent contradictions—action, nonaction; violence, nonviolence. His understanding of karma-yoga, or union with God through action, stands out in underlined passages in the copy of the Bhagavad Gita that he meditated with.

The room restored by the Canadian brought back memories of Merton and his death, and the wooden ceilings brought back Keats. There was a ferocious tenacity to the wood in contrast to the time frame granted to a human being. The wood would outlast the monk, unless, as with Merton, fire took it away. The rooms gave the Canadian a practice to follow. But in their concrete, material form, the connection he sought was not found. The forest in the knotted pine remained an unspeaking desert. It was painful, dry, and the flow of history, its power to dominate, and wreck and deny, to wither, while human beings grew frightened, was present in the room.

There was beauty in his work, but his heart was not satisfied. The wood lasted, but lasting wasn't enough. The work demonstrated the humble fact that one is always a beginner who knows nearly nothing of the scope of religious life. The monk felt that he needed to connect with something of more living consequence. He needed to move into a present where he could touch others. He needed morning, too, to find him, warming his sense of purpose in his barely tended garden.

"To work alone you are entitled, never to its fruit. Neither let your motive be the fruit of action, nor let your attachment be to non-action." Merton had underlined that passage in the Bhagavad Gita. The Canadian understood that passage, I'm quite certain. It means that life is the reward, without answers, but with knowledge that night and day, good and evil, God and the void are present in every breath one takes. His humility and sincerity in living as a Christian monk were palpable, as palpable as the difficulties.

XXVII

Memory Again

They reveal the tight bindings of early instruction and a time capsule
that no photo can capture.

1

So much was planted in me in the Rome years. Some events simply thrilled a midwesterner. Often they were discoveries of innocuous loopholes in social conditioning that made breathing easier or more spontaneous. They astound me for how they magnify a persona. They reveal the tight bindings of early instruction and a time capsule that no photo can capture. They present themselves as little mannerisms, but they carry the heavy weight of expectations for a woman's behavior.

The first time I inspected a glass shelf of fried doughnuts in a bar near my little house in Rome was at least as groundbreaking as my first kiss. The epiphany happened rather fast, soon after the barman asked me which one I would like. Let's be clear: I was wearing a long skirt, conforming to the way I was expected to look in Rome at that time. But I was far away from the place where I had been trained to pick up feminine cues. I was physically outside of the reach of training that cost me something when I felt that I had offended.

The doughnuts were of unfairly different sizes. The barman's dark eyes relished that. Tongue-tied by manners and automatically assuming that the girl should choose the worst, since there were men and children who would want what I selfishly wanted, I rested my eyes on a smallish one. Snatching the largest doughnut with steel pincers, extracting it like an amphora in an excavation, the Roman laughed as he made a ceremony of setting it down on a plate decorated with a napkin. "Here," he said a bit condescendingly, as if he were coaching a younger sister, helping her to get on in the world. "This is the best one. The only choice." The first greasy bite tasted like a U.S. Supreme Court decision that challenged the basis of society.

In that bite, I can extrapolate forward to explanations of why we deserve or need or should congratulate ourselves for taking something that modesty or altruism might have censored. While it is difficult to think that merely snatching things out from under the competing eyes of others is progress, I shall always treasure the Roman's gesture that normalized a basic fact: It is human to want things.

In university, I often flailed without understanding the precise problem that was upsetting me. In a blue-book exam about *Sense and Sensibility*, by Jane Austen, I resisted praising the book and compared Austen's work to Dostoyevsky's, making her viewpoint emerge as shallow. I poured out pages about the premises that formed identity in her characters—social status, money, limits created by family relationships of jealousy and falsity. Since those issues felt so unbearable to me, so confining, so unfair, I went on to explain why the Russian writer's work contained more depth and thus was a more legitimate way not only to live but to see character and write about it.

My professor called me in and explained that I could not write such things and expect to pass. I agreed with him, shed tears while explaining my doubts about and resentments of Austen. He loaned me an immaculate handkerchief, lifting it from his suit coat pocket, shaking its folds open like a little parachute, while he, a brilliant, fastidious scholar, continued to listen. The next day when he entered our room, he was pale; I would even say haggard. "Class," he said, "I am returning your blue books. I was unable to grade them. I had a ghastly night and didn't shut my eyes. You see, someone raised questions I had never thought about before, and now, although I've always held her in the highest esteem, I don't know what I think about Jane Austen."

XXVIII

The Market

Then, perhaps, crates of artichokes, thorns thrusting from long, stiff stems. Next dazzling lemons. Lemons, rough and large as breasts on Roman statues.

1

The market that was three hundred meters from the courtyard overflowed with the seasonal appearance of all that was so reasonably available to everyone. Partially stored in the courtyard, the market erupted every day in the Campo de' Fiori. The iron wheels of the carts that would display the produce rumbled over the stones leading in and out of the arch. The cellars that kept the fruit and vegetables cool were padlocked each evening and unlocked before dawn even in winter.

Then, it never reached my mind to ask where the sellers obtained their produce. They must have collected it from a central market, the way I did later on in northern Italy, where for two summers I helped with archaeological digs and worked alongside a country woman to prepare two meals a day for the forty-person crew. In the central market where I bought the basic materials I needed each day, goods were sold in bulk between 5:00 and 7:00 a.m. Although I was never asked for identification, presumably there is a network that services merchants and wholesalers.

So I have no real sense of how the produce got to the courtyard carts in the first place. But I do remember well the variety of things that those rugged people offered. Tomatoes were gold, red-gold: little pumpkin shapes, or shaped like pears, or round and shiny as Ping-Pong balls, or attached to others with starlike stems. Besides selecting one type or another according to its use, there were other choices to be considered: ripe, very ripe, or still half green and able to last on a nonrefrigerated shelf.

Next to tomatoes, basil was wedged in: branches of it, wafting a slightly aniselike scent. Clumps had been pulled up before they went to seed and usually were lashed in bunches, occasionally sprouting small yellow-and-white flowers. The abundant bouquets made one feel slightly drugged and very rich as two or three heaps were stuffed in string bags.

"Basil" is a poem I have written every year since I lived in Rome and it still falls short. I try and am still patiently waiting for the click of an image to release its essence.

> The scent has no lid
> the midnight place
> comes from its dizzying
> leaves

2

In the Campo market, alongside the tomatoes and basil, was salad, often sandy, muddy, and tender green. Next to its varieties were radicchio, with its shocking purple tones and dirty roots still

attached, then endive and bitter-tasting chicory. Then, perhaps, crates of artichokes, thorns thrusting from long, stiff stems. Next dazzling lemons. Lemons, rough and large as breasts on Roman statues. Bright lemons with evergreen leaves, piled up near blood oranges, many of which were cut and exposed like deep rubies. Grapes, the moscato kind, went on and on down the planks, large bunches heaped on large bunches, each grape carrying that extraordinary translucent film that made them look tarnished.

White garlic came in braids of twenty or thirty bulbs. They vied with red onions, green onions, white onions, and chives. There were bananas, but they were frowned upon as being imperialist, with their blue labels: Chiquita. Potatoes were sold with their soil attached. Eggs, often smeared with blood, were taken from bowls and eventually wrapped in newspaper, one by one. If they had been found that morning, porcini mushrooms, as large as baby bonnets, were kept under the counter and pulled out, the way the thieves on the corner pulled out stolen watches. Zucchini flowers, yellow blossoms, to be fried, appeared for a month or so. In fact, the entire market emptied and filled and changed produce with the seasons in the Mediterranean, which were always interesting and generous.

The market in the late sixties groaned with produce that was organic and within anyone's reach. The market people sold one orange if that was what was wanted or all that could be afforded. Or two luscious figs, still oozing with sugar. Or they gave away a bag of apples or lettuce starting to wilt. The rusting scales that can be seen in ancient Roman frescoes and found in tomb paintings where the soul waits to be weighed hung from the rafters of old canvas umbrellas. Using combinations of brass measures to tilt them, workers totaled up the costs. Much produce was not weighed, but offered, without cost, because otherwise it would have been wasted. There was a strong sense of sharing, driven in part by perishability, by rot. Food was alive. Nothing was measured in literal weights or amounts. *Mangia. Mangia.* Eat. Eat. Every day except Sunday, the market was rolled out and set down before seven and folded up and rolled back into the courtyard before two.

3

Touching the market's abundance and glories makes other memories surface. My intention is to turn toward a conclusion, to use food as another way of delving into culture here, and how skepticism and inertia can be vital and healthy. But now the thieves have jostled me. Just by describing mushrooms being sold under the counter like stolen watches, I see the connection. I cannot avoid mentioning the thieves who lived on the corner of my street and its junction with the Cancelleria and the market in Campo de' Fiori.

The thieves fit their roles physically, dressed in baggy clothes, shifting from one foot to the other, giving the impression that they had nothing to do as they stood at the corner. By and large, they were petty thieves, pickpockets and even scavengers. Once in a while, though, like magpies, if they spotted treasures in cars, usually parked for Vatican events, they might manage a bigger haul if they could chance upon the right combination of confusion and distraction.

Here are two or three stories to flesh out an ambivalence that illustrates, one more time, what complicity is and does. The thieves,

a group of heavyset men, prematurely aged, spied a fur coat in the backseat of the car of one of my students. She had a large furniture store on the Corso Vittorio Emanuele and was a friend of Gian Carlo Menotti, the man who founded the Festival of the Two Worlds in Spoleto. Stepping into the courtyard, her jeweled arms and tight dresses usually brought all the people in the windows to a respectful silence as she climbed the stairs. However, once the Roman equivalent of the Blues Brothers saw the full-length leopard-skin coat spread out on the backseat of her Lancia, they pounced. When she finished her hour, her coat, so vast that it probably had been made from two or three whole poached pelts, had been hoisted by the locals.

It was enough for her to tell me this and to offer a ten-thousand-lire reward, and the collective community went into action. Chagrined, I stood at the corner, speaking in a loud, studied voice to a market person.

"And she will give ten thousand lire for its return. No questions asked."

"Poor woman. Poor us. Poor Italians that we steal."

We continued speaking as the little group of men circled.

Within the hour, one of them climbed the stairs, carrying the spectacular coat, while Rosina cried out, "*Grazie al cielo.* Thank heavens it's been found."

When friends with a camper that they had driven all the way from India parked it in the same booby-trapped place, another of the thieves knocked on the door. He stepped to the rim of my stairs and spoke to the figures in the windows, as if he were confiding his prologue to the audience.

"There is a camper out in the parking lot that is bulging with too much irresistible stuff. I have heard that thieves are hanging around. I heard someone say that if all that booty stays where it is, they will break in just to show the people how stupid they are. That's what I heard. I don't know if it's true. But I've come to tell you that you should remove the temptation."

Like clowns that keep exiting a small car, the last story is about my visit to the police, when I asked about the thieves and why they were not caught and punished. My stance was logical and full of the indignation of a person who believes she knows how things should be run, who carries cultural training from a foreign home.

The answer, in that Roman face expressing slight fatigue, came from a heavyset man who had his own answers about how his district functioned.

"We know who they are. If we bother them, they will just move to another place, like the rats. This way, they know that we know and that keeps everything within bounds. No violence. We pretend to shut our eyes. They don't steal from the locals. Do you get me? Everything's under control."

4

The poet William Carlos Williams believed in the truth in things. This book is about Italy, and if it is also about me, it is, as was announced, about the river, memory as a presence that is fluidly part of the present. It is about the persistence of physical history and how it shapes a mind: beauty and truth, eyes, hands, feet, and the heart always coming up against and meeting time and its effects. The stories told about that kind of time usually, in part, mirror something of the conceivable and inconceivable. Italy offers itself as a place to discover life that is both beautiful and difficult because of immobility. It is a place that suggests that reality is where one can never assume that it will be possible to live entirely by one's code. Life is boundless and yet one will be bound by limits that will force denial, compromise, and recognition of emptiness that will give ritual its abundance. Community is necessary for survival and for defining equality and equal chance.

5

For me as a writer, words have always enveloped fascination but also pain that is nearly pure. Growing up as a midwestern child with Protestant parents, I bumped into many walls in words. I had enough space in childhood to play and to play with the words I knew, starting from the magnified silence of isolation, being punished or isolated for saying what I thought. Even mild conflict was defined as disturbing and disturbing the peace. But those rules were quite clear. And, like most children, one talked to oneself and then ran along and played outside.

But these were not the only walls. I adored my brothers (my sister was years from being born), and I tagged and trailed along, not allowed to do what they did, whether it was subjects studied or games played. Females didn't need math. Girls needed sewing kits, while the boys got Erector sets. But that, too, might have been passed off as what hung in the air as dismal social norms. But the concept of female for both my parents was fraught with emotional contradictions. The reality for me of being one was more or less a constant battle. While I do not doubt their love, I experienced an enormous set of problems working around what seemed like double nets. Both parents defined problems they had by assigning them to me. They both continued spiraling in, so that it was difficult for me to make the inside and the outside of my life into one thing.

My father took on the task of rewriting what I wrote. He had written a large number of political speeches, and his language tended to have that pitch. There was no way for me to write without his version appearing. Turning his adult versions down, defending my own work, which already seemed to have hollow sides to it, I rarely reached the words that expressed my voiceless half.

So silence in the house most often had a color like lead. *Peace* was a word that broke in two chambers, one false and repressed and the other vast and to be explored. Yet from the beginning, there were other views in the house. Though we were not allowed to have friends in, we still hardly lived in a dungeon. As children, we were read children's stories, undoubtedly for far too long, and were free to go outside, unsupervised, to bicker and barter, put on plays, read comic books, and surreptitiously breach rules. There were apple trees to be climbed, backyards to be crossed by slipping under fences. There were streams with crabs and ice that froze hard enough to skate on. We had space and could lie on hills, rolling down them, or looking up at the sky, which was never boring or narrow. Four distinct seasons marked so many experiences and sensations. In their unfolding, they spread out perceptions of enormous and majestic. We were free to bumble off to the public library, and there in that association of smells—musty pages, slight grime, linoleum—something real, human, emerged. Unlike anything in the house, it seemed that this might be the smell of truth.

Snow was the best embodiment of silence, especially when a blizzard lasted for days, bringing beauty and stillness to the yards and trees, halting the few cars that managed to climb the hills. When we were children, we played freely on sleds, until our wet snow clothes began to freeze. As a teen, a walk at night with the clear stars and bright moonlight above would show one's booted feet leaving a trail that wiped out the pristine state. Each step was a soft sound. Those night skies, often accompanied by the smell of wet wool, were pitched with the indigo reembraced around Duccio's Madonna in Siena.

Walks on freezing nights were never frightening. Looking up at stars was liberation. If the walk was disturbing, it was only because of the effect we have on things. The imprints of my fur-lined snow boots captured me when I was small. They were company in some ways, and yet early on, they left me with a consciousness of having intruded. In that sensation, I can feel my child's sense of worry, and my parents' admonitions. But the experience also gave me an image and a model for something that matters. By touching things, we alter them. The reality fits well with why writing has always seemed a pact.

6

The memories of my young self keep pressing. One event that makes me laugh aloud, now that I am trying to remember the person I was at age twenty-six, occurred one morning as I walked to the Tiber to give my morning salute.

In the crammed little Via Gubonari, a young man on a Vespa passed close by me, and I felt the purse hanging by a strap on my shoulder caught and tugged. My shoulder was yanked. My thoughts thrashed with the midwestern teachings I had been given for facing life. *I have caught my purse on his motorbike. What if he falls? It is my fault that he will be hurt.* That rush of guilt was as good as adrenaline to snap me to attention. Without thinking, my long legs altruistically picked up speed and I shouted while keeping up, "Watch out, watch out. You might fall. My purse is caught on your Vespa." He turned and could not believe that I was running alongside. He began shouting "Let go, let go." He did not accelerate fully, and I kept up for more than half a block as we weaved back and forth, each holding to our tether. At a certain point, others noticed. He sensed he could be trapped. Flying hard, the bag hurled back to me as he sped off in a cloud of face-saving declamation that involved, as in all Italian curses, an insult to one's mother.

From the outside view (the opinion of those hypothetical neighbors whom my mother used as the rhetorical ombudsmen to regulate our manners), it must have seemed to him as if I had nerve that would cause him trouble. To the people who gathered around me, I was brave. I was a young American woman, modern as Jane Fonda. *Che coraggio.* The gap was the desert I was still trying to cross. I seldom saw danger when I thought I should help. I saw most situations that went wrong as being my fault, and for that reason I was stubbornly attracted to experiences that broke the bell jar of childhood while I continued to fear feelings of being at fault.

There had been no wars surrounding us in the suburbs. There was no want. And we talked; in fact, that was nearly all we did. And we talked in such a way that words were equated with intelligence. And yet, talk was about the narrowest range of things. There were signs and messages that said not to disturb the mostly uncontested sense of order—between men and women, between inferiority and superiority, between bodies and minds, countries, science and religion. And how did words link to action?

Many words had double or triple meanings that remained unspoken to avoid tampering with the black box of assumptions. So much of the forties and fifties at a national and world level was steeped in secrecy and silence; so many people accepted given definitions of difference, repression, hierarchy. In some people's views now, those times look nostalgically ordered, and the values look humane. But on the whole, the world has taken infinite forward steps since then, especially in breaking silences. To break a silence is a serious act, simple and so complicated, because it is only the first step in things breaking.

Who is to say what that run alongside the thief meant? Who can link it to what came before? It does, in any case, make a fine story—those long legs that ran were useful, as they have been on many other occasions. Certainly that is what should be remembered. After all, I saved my purse. And for the rest, it was another instance where I had not even imagined danger, and that makes it more difficult to judge, since the premises were all wrong.

7

Rome is memory: the way it breaks down, and yet remains, in others' memories, drawings, notebooks, bricks fired centuries ago. It is about the burden of memory, the futility of it, and relief that much disappears and what remains can be winnowed, or selected for new meanings. It is about the absolute importance of others and other times, all that has been lived, lost, accepted in order to find a place in our times. Memory is large, important like marble. Made banal, used for personal grievances and invented events, it makes a mockery of itself, of memory's capacity to reach over time and cast sharp, contrasting light.

8

The mailman brought letters twice a day in those years. He puttered in on a motorbike and would call out my name. Without phones or the Internet, the mail was an event. The way life offered feelings of novelty in those days was a beautiful thing. Choices matured and the prospects contained in them offered plenty of time for musing and exploration. Letters contained feelings that had been thought about and were imagined to last longer than it took a letter to arrive. Letters mused and considered ideas, and poured out deeply private things, meant only for one pair of eyes. Sealed. The little package of a letter meant an exchange of deliberation and focus, if not always elegance and truth.

A letter had come from England and I had been out. Rosina was alarmed, and in the discussions that had ensued, no one could sign for it. Since I thought it concerned my marriage, I went to the central post office, hoping I could retrieve it.

The story is really Italian and embodies what I loved about Rome. In a stereotypical way, this attitude of flexibility causes northern Italians to believe in the myth of their own superiority. The retrieval window was closed. The post office was pulling down its external metal shutters, but I insisted that I desperately needed the letter, and they bent. They broke many postal rules.

I followed a woman who was already wearing her jacket to go home for lunch as we went into the innards of the post office, where we navigated around piles and stacks of letters all to be sorted by hand. The room looked like a desperately understaffed dry cleaner's with its daunting heaps and bundles. Taking up my cause, two or three clerks began lifting sacks and scrambling through them. They found the letter after twenty minutes of stirring and dropping. A desire to help pushed them on.

The immediately empathetic response, their willingness to create chaos to address a need, undoubtedly symbolizes the healing spell of those years. If I add that the letter I tore open there created problems for those who broke the rules, I am describing my chagrin. I dropped the envelope on the floor as I rushed out to read a letter of what would be only more excuses.

In the afternoon, the *postino* brought a communication from the head of the post office, summoning me.

I reviewed how I had broken the law. I thought of my self-centeredness. I imagined that I might be in trouble. The following morning, when I faced the director in his worn-out official hat with unfaded braid, he held a torn envelope high and then tossed it on the desk.

"We Italians are the laughingstock of the world. Everyone considers us thieves," he said abjectly. "I found this on the floor. I'm ashamed to say it was empty. How much money were you expecting?"

"May I see the envelope?" I asked.

The handwriting had not changed from the day before.

"There was no money," I said.

The official lessened his frown. His face relaxed a little.

"I opened it. I'm so sorry." Then I must have made a face at the handwriting, slanted, determined, and yet oddly irregular, which I knew as well as my own.

The official's eyes met mine. They were amused, relieved. The mystery had been resolved. Italy's honor had emerged clean.

He stepped to the other side of his desk. He patted my shoulder, as if he understood perfectly the gist of the event. He chose to ignore the circumstances that had allowed me to penetrate the inner workings of the post office in the first place. The investigation was closed. "I'm very sorry," he said with a mild shrug.

Why am I telling this? Because it shows how human judgment guided matters to a solution. It shows kindness, a sense of humor, tolerance without moralizing. It shows how things swing. How stones, once they are known to be solid, allow for life to flow richly around them.

XXIX

Truth Is Beauty, Beauty Truth

Thou shalt remain, in midst of other woe
Than ours . . .

—John Keats

1

Because Italy cultivates the past as an element of complexity and mediation, the past remains a sack that can never be emptied. Its ever-changing solidity keeps one in bounds. There is no absolute belief in progress, although its trudge forward is unmistakable.

Italy is a story that always starts with "In the beginning there was already something before what you think is the beginning." In the beginning there was the Word, but the mind came before. In the beginning there was man, but there was a goddess who birthed man. Yes, you were born, but so were your mother and father, your grandfather and grandmother. Italy is a complex story of anything you want bounded by what others want. That is why traffic is such a creative and active challenge.

2

The dialectic of middle-class Protestant families, or at least ours in the Midwest, was based on stability and the ability to push hard in resistance, knowing that the structure was made up of solid old pillars, albeit unforgiving ones. Doubt and uncertainty belonged to the young and never passed the sealed lips of the elders. Continuity and unchanging values were offered by my parents—and offered with all their insistent and sincere love that we were their most important focus.

It was probably the absolute blow of our father's death that broke the seal of a constricted model. In the suburbs, death was put away, an anomaly to be folded up like a washed permanent-press sheet. Death, in our family, was often talked about as a new start for those who remained. Its reality was a secret.

We lived in a neighborhood where people's assumptions more or less conformed to the ideas of whites who tacitly accepted segregation in the first half of America's twentieth century, and often explicitly wrote it into restrictive private charters. People drawn to such arrangements were not drawn to any sort of unwilled sharing. We had neighbors, but there was no mingling among those who lived in large and separated yards, ample plots cut from a beer manufacturer's land in the nineteenth century and then populated by families with manufacturing bases—the founder of Harley-Davidson, the president of Allis Chalmers, an international producer of agricultural machines, the president of a large regional paint company, the founder of a national root beer company—nor was showing real need for help or affection encouraged in our immediate family. Optimism covered things over and kept the expression of problems, sorrow, confusion, or differences far from conversation. In general, then, the suburban model we experienced was actually about life in suspension, formal, with privilege providing an illusion of living not only outside urban mixtures of complexity and tough going but outside life's tragedies and pain, as well. Confusion, stumbling, anger did not exist among those selected to reside there—at least in the way our mother insisted life be lived.

A week after my father's death, my mother assumed I would go back to Pittsburgh, take a long bus ride to its inner city, where I was working with the Quakers in the slums. "Why stay here? There's nothing more to do." My response was obvious: "We need each other. I can't leave. How will we deal with the changes? We need to give each other support. We need to cry. There's pain, Mom." I can still see her shaking her head and making a face as if I were crazy, as if death and the loss of a father, a husband, a fabric of dependence built up among four children was a bewildering effect that needed to be quickly put back in order. She clearly was lost. Out went his books, those on the Renaissance, with their lessons of perspective, once kept off-limits on the highest shelves of his library; out went his suits, his shoes, his tools, all given to people like the milkman; out went my desk, out went the pool, the cars, the house, until she physically erased that life and squeezed into an apartment so small that her four children could never be there at the same time.

3

Even the stranger, the foreigner, the exile fits into the collective memory of Rome, where members of the newly conquered kingdoms could become Roman citizens by accepting certain tenets. For me, living in the courtyard was like joining an extended family. It offered the stability and openness of a family where plenty meant sharing. Communication had limits, but it wasn't confounded by artificial reactions defined by books on manners, abstractions about the limits of women, or messages of competition.

Helping each other was a possibility. The courtyard was a micro-cosm of city life, with tastes and smells, conflicts, and modest aspi-rations. It reeked with the freedom of sharing life and opinions. It had rats and fights and faith existing in a tacit state of tolerance. As people said their prayers out loud and nodded to each other, they called out before they went to bed:

"*Buona notte, Io.*"

"*Buona notte, Lucia.*"

"*Buona notte, Rosina.*"

Human voices went around the yard, from window to win-dow, before lights snapped out. The insomniacs, who had TVs, turned them up louder then while they sat in the dark, waiting to fall asleep in front of the blaring screen. How much more do I need to write to spell out how much good the courtyard did me?

XXX

Pentimento

Pentimento means a change of mind.

1

I first saw pentimenti in Rome when I was doing translations for an agent insuring art in the Vatican. He had a briefcase of X-rays, which he spread out on the table in my little courtyard living room as he sifted through the medical-size gray-and-black images. Each painting was being X-rayed in order to make an assessment of its worth. "The question is, usually," he said, "does this discovery make it more valuable? Since it is seldom better than the final result, the issue of destroying what covered it is generally not an issue.

"Here," he said, holding up an X-ray against the lamp, "you see the painter changed his mind about the arm. He brought it to the young man's side. That made the painter place the sword on the ground. That changed the vertical thrust and added horizontal emphasis. We'd never have known that without our process of investigation."

2

Pentimento means a change of mind. Whether it means regret or a positive decision, it refers to taking an image and altering it—covering it over, or removing part of it—in order to improve upon the whole. It is a fairly common part of the process of creation. Caravaggio in the Contarelli Chapel made such interventions in major ways on the canvas of The Martyrdom of Saint Matthew.

What the viewer sees as the painting with Saint Matthew as the central focus was the artist's ultimate intent. It is the task of researchers and restorers to reconstruct the events that led to the final result.

The pentimento is a gesture of process, of doubt, of consciousness, intuition that led the artist to understand what would make the composition strong or sublime. *This was the plan, but when I saw it, I knew that it needed to be changed. Just move the vase a few inches to the right. Change the figure who is sleeping to one who is awake.* Deliberation, yes, but a forward action toward a better solution. In the strokes called pentimento, something will disappear or be destroyed. But the oxides will tell tales. The strokes will still caress the canvas as slight eruptions. Even if you ended up painting a completely different picture, some curious person could find the contradictions in how you had arrived at the result.

3

Pentimento is surely part of memory, one image replaced by another, event or experience, perhaps consciously, perhaps the result of a traumatic erasure. Dreams are looked at for pentimenti, underlying realities that reappear and need space or integration in the present. Italy, everywhere, suggests this process, this human act of covering and yet not completely erasing. Writing in a narrative voice does, as well. Are the colors right? Do you need a horizontal thrust? In covering an image over, or uncovering it, what happens to the composition? An artist's pentimenti are full of ambiguities. Usually it is conjecture as to what they mean, except that the acts were meant to correct.

Pentimento. Pentimenti. Four beats as soft as only Italian words can be while presenting so many consonants. In the description of the act of consciously covering, there is the human condition, trying to get things right but needing many starts. The word can be tinged with regret, an admission of mistakes. Often the corrections are slight and the reasons obvious.

Anyone who undertakes to write by using memories knows the sobering realization that one is confined to a medium in which one page follows the next. The shape and the composition are not a single unified canvas, but, rather, a riot and steady stream of impressions where beauty and truth vie for order as they face the waves and dancing light of years and years. The reality of pentimenti.

XXXI

Epigenetics and Ferragosto

For many years, I thought that Ferragosto, the high holiday of empty streets, the fifteenth of August, was another form, like fire drills, for practicing civic preparedness.

1

The idea of latent versus real potential has always appealed to me. What is unknown, in every breath, in every moment, is far greater than what our fearful minds can allow us to entertain. Sometimes an attitude of open acceptance becomes the right ground for a new root. In the space of a few months, I participated in three conversations about epigenetics, a way of analyzing environmental influence on genes, that revealed an exhilarating coil of associations that linked my thoughts to Ferragosto, a centuries-old Italian *festa*.

2

I have more memories of Ferragosto than I would like to admit. It is the day when cities look like de Chirico's paintings. For many years, I thought that Ferragosto, the high holiday of empty streets, the fifteenth of August, was another form, like fire drills, for practicing civic preparedness. On that holiday, anyone left in an Italian city works out what would happen if there were an atomic blast and no one to direct operations. How would they survive and manage to find a bar that was open, or a newspaper stand? After milling around in frustration, the victims would find their way to the hospital. On the most deserted day of the year, medical staffs would brush up skills needed for people with panic attacks caused by having been abandoned.

3

Ferragosto is usually boiling hot. The shutters with their padlocks are all down, so that, under beating sun, the only echoes of human life are protests from tourists and their children. The smart and prosperous residents are at the sea or in the mountains. Immigrants, with no extra money, sit in the parks and, at night, listen to radios or sing.

Yet if I am being objective and want to use an analogy, in recent years if Ferragosto represented the inherited holiday, a fixed point of metropolitan apnea, then the environment, as revealed by epigenetics, was always inherent in the feast day. Over centuries, epigenetics has influenced the cultural inheritances of this holiday, then and now bringing forth other elements that were not immediately apparent. Ferragosto once was a day when everyone congregated in cities and churches.

4

In Rome, an Australian woman, whom I knew vaguely, was hit by a runaway driver on Ferragosto. I was asked to go to the central hospital to help. She gave the ambulance attendant my address and they found my stairs, asked me to assist, since she was alone. The hospital worker waited until I collected my things. Landlines in those days sometimes took years to install, and cell phones were not even science fiction. Relatives and friends were the ones in hospitals to carry bedpans and find palatable food. So it wasn't unusual that an employee came looking for me.

The Australian's memory had been temporarily altered. Her arm was broken and she had been put in a teeming ward for observation. The windows were wide open and flies buzzed. There were critical accident victims on stretchers and no aisles to speak of.

There was no breeze, and the sound levels were not surprising, given the number of patients and relatives. The Australian's head was wrapped with a bandage that made her look like a sweating pirate. And since she had no one she could reach to help her, we spent the day in the hospital together, with me swatting flies and answering questions about where she was and why.

"It's Ferragosto," I said.

"Ferragosto?"

"A holiday."

"What kind of holiday is this?" she asked, trying to pull her bloody bandage from her head. "A *festa* for flies?"

"A huge holiday that shuts everything down."

"What kind of holiday?" she moaned, pointing to the person in the bed next to hers, who was drawing his last breaths. I had no answer for that and still regret that I did nothing to help the man, who, too, was terribly alone. He struggled with his sheet before he died in a state of great agitation, pulling his legs up, so that they were draped like a white mountain.

In Parma, we saw the emergency room for the major part of Ferragosto when a friend slipped playing Frisbee and had to be taken in and placed in a line of people who had endured roughly comparable disasters. The room throbbed with a few major problems, and the rest of the patients seemed to have complaints like indigestion from food that went bad in the heat or slamming a finger in a drawer. Many struck out at family members who had abandoned them. I felt very fortunate that our friend, with his broken elbow, was British. He certainly didn't complain, and the atmosphere made him marvel at how Italy, in spite of everything, manages to work. The little white net they finally put on his arm was ingenious. The staff had no interest in doing the paperwork to charge him. "Jolly good," he said, pleased that the eight hours of cultural immersion and Italian largesse had not cost a single lira.

5

Although I told the Australian that the holiday was an important one, it took me nearly twenty years before I realized that the deadest point in the entire Italian year, Ferragosto, was actually a feast day to celebrate the assumption of Mary. Like many festivals, its origins were multiple, the first being in 18 B.C.E., when the emperor Augustus declared Feriae Augusti. The Catholic Church officially made the date dogma in the nineteenth century when they claimed it for Mary, who, conceived without sin, physically rises, body and soul, into heaven on that day. By the time I discovered that Ferragosto had this miraculous significance, I no longer heard my father's or mother's voice telling me that Mary and all those trappings had nothing to do with Christian doctrine. The *festa* rolled in: empty streets, very few signs of religious processions, and yet, the whole of Italy, north to south, was somewhere feasting, lying on a beach or sweating behind dark shutters, because people since the Middle Ages had wanted Mary to be settled, fairly and logically, in heaven.

It made a difference to me, once I knew that every upward draft in paintings where Mary is ascending is actually depicting a day that is usually windless. In the Parma cathedral, where Mary is waiting to ascend, you can feel the mightiness of the turbine winds. Cosmic forces were thrown in to give important energies to the myth of parity. The assumption of Mary completes and authenticates the claim not so much of an equal role, but, rather, the obvious fact that women, spiritually and physically, are central to all of life.

6

I would need to devote far more space to the complexity and the sparseness of what is known about epigenetics if I were to be serious about describing it. Instead, it was the sheer coincidence of hearing three discussions about it, one in the United States, one in Italy, and one in England, that excited me. It was enough to conclude the topic was in the air.

Analogy can be dangerous in using figures of speech to describe mechanisms in science. Words can make things easy to understand, but they may have little to do with what scientists are telling us. One of the great gaps of our century is that we laypeople know next to nothing about many of the great and beautiful languages of our century, the languages of science. We will never possess the preparation needed to get us there. We tend to diminish the mysteries that most scientists conceive of as mysteries, which we grasp only as pale approximations.

7

The first conversation about epigenetics was initiated by a nephew after a memorial service for my mother, who died suddenly at age ninety-five. He and I had shared a brief lyrical moment, after a meal, when he pointed out a perfect tiny blue finch dead on the terrace. The freezing, bright May winds were blustery, picking up things, dropping them, smashing. We exchanged quick glances, as if this exquisite bird was a sign of her. She would have wept at its beauty and the fact that it was dead. So mysterious, unusual, out of place, it fit with our shy mention of birds as symbols for souls. After four years of uncomplaining withdrawal into dementia, her final years were essences of the dignity she had wished to teach us. The touchingly beautiful bird expressed something that we wanted to understand.

My nephew, a thriving artist, in part because he asks interesting questions, probed my husband about the influence of environment on genetics. The family gathering stimulated that. By way of response, in the classical didactic method of many Italian professors, my husband asked the young artist to give his explanation for this field. The artist said, "I think that epigenetics is a line of studies giving as much weight to the environment influencing genetic inheritance as to the actual genetic code. The genome [the genetic inheritance] and the epigenome [the system that can influence when and how genes are turned off and on] are now providing a far more nuanced explanation of how an individual develops and acts."

"Very good." My husband gave him a broad smile. My tendency to look for influences has always made me focus on the external environment, family, culture. For me, epigenetics carried intriguing implications, and many had to do with the way culture defines identity. When does a person become him- or herself if the environment can trigger new responses in the brain? Can what we have inherited biologically be thought of as a potluck feast where there is always room for more dishes? That day, we settled on a metaphor for inheritance. Each person—genome and

epigenome—was so vast and so partially known that we might as well see ourselves as galaxies.

8

In the conversation I was part of in Parma, in between the roast potatoes and the freshly harvested green salad, the questions were: What is an identity in a largely plastic and developing being? Is it from the moment of conception? When does the soul enter this inheritance that can be altered, even before birth, by others acting on it? Is the concept of inheritance the one that is limiting? Or is the idea of a fundamentally fixed identity the culprit and more confining—that is, little Guilio is some sort of locked genetic essence from the beginning?

When the conversation expanded to the soul, it seemed to have been inspired by the wine and the beauty of the stars. It was surprising to me that a Marxist brought the topic up, but not in a polemical way. Perhaps he felt the need to seize the unusual convergence of a physicist, a psychologist, a yoga teacher, and an engineer, as well as a writer and a biologist, to pose a question that did not usually emerge among his circle of colleagues.

Someone asked, it seemed to me a bit rhetorically, if a person was altered, was the soul altered? Then a more technical question: If the mother's blood influenced the child, was the fetus ever truly itself? I must say that it was a perfect August evening, except for bands of persistent mosquitoes. The food didn't get cold, but it was forgotten on the plates for a considerable period of time. The conversation itself was chaotic and looking for definition to be pulled from the speculations.

In London, at a conference on life narratives and human rights, where I gave a paper on Primo Levi's delineation of the gray zone in human responses, a neurologist talked about mapping the brain and how little is known about it. Yet he was encouraged by the new imaging technologies that were identifying its parts and their uses. The brain responds to voluntary as well as involuntary signals. The many signals touch areas primed to respond, but as experiences change, the brain, which has a vast array of responses, will be stimulated to use them. These changing responses fit into another side of epigenetics. When and how do these responses call on unused parts of genes to express themselves and thus open new paths in the same brain or cell? Does any potential for peace lie in that direction?

9

So where and why am I thinking about Ferragosto, which I didn't know existed when I grew up? I didn't know what it meant even long after I had lived in Italy. Many Italians don't remember the Church origins of Ferragosto. Why is a holiday celebrating Mary's assumption experienced as desertion now?

When we realize that the mother figure is no longer imagined as a woman without sin, but, instead, as one who might be found at the beach and not cooking, what has happened to Mary's influence, the archetypal image that moves us so profoundly? In ever greater numbers, new Italian arrivals remain in the city, and some of the Chinese and North Africans try to keep shops open in that period of closures. Perhaps Ferragosto still exists as deserted streets, but now that generalization is no longer powerfully true. The living part of Ferragosto is expressing something that is changing. Is the environment bringing this about? It's a holiday made of notes that are played but also those that are unplayed.

So this is what seems to be the link. I have been driven by feelings of hope and grief—overwhelmed since my mother's death by so many memories and questions that have to do with unknowing, with complexities that curl in every direction as I remember my childhood and its enormous stabilities.

Our lives were offered to us by our parents, who gave us their genes and shepherded us along. Our genes themselves are laden with potentials, even potentials different from appearances. Ferragosto and epigenetics are alive with questions about change, influence, memory, past, and present. Every single life, even one as exquisite and small and articulated as the blue finch's, reaches, only in a way, something like an end. Its secrets pull like wings.

XXXII

Slow Food

Why run?

—Primo Levi, "The Snail" (translated by Wallis Wilde-Menozzi)

1

Food has not always been plentiful in Italy. Coming up from Sicily, the Allies encountered starvation and malnourishment everywhere. The second-largest land reform in Europe took place in Italy in 1950, when sharecropping essentially came to an end. Especially in the south, packets of land, not necessarily economically viable or sound, were redistributed. Large holdings from absentee landlords were broken up, and often it was cooperatives reflecting social and economic realities that tried to organize ways to make agriculture work. The cooperative movement in food production has grown into one of the most successful economic and social organizations in Italy, especially in the north, where their supermarkets are the largest Italian-owned chain. Their products carry extra messages, like the recent offer of wines from Mafia-confiscated lands. The wines are named after victims and martyrs such as Placido Rizzotto, a union organizer in Sicily in the 1940s who disappeared and whose remains were recently found. Co-ops generally market local produce, indicating additives and production methods. They support large networks of small farmers.

Food, especially in times of scarcity, was, as my husband remembers, held sacred and shared. Food preparation was an activity for women, which they participated in collectively each and every day. But precisely because it was overseen as work, from the polenta that was ground from corn and stirred to the tinned *sgombro* prepared in response to the Catholic Church's rule for eating fish on Friday, the ritual of food never ceased following the seasons and honoring what was found, was raised, or was bought in measured purchases. Because food provided entertainment as well as nourishment, pleasure, and company, its preparation was a drama of conducting and saving, elaborating on notes and remembering from fantasies recipes to reconstruct. The lap was always open. The power in pasta, in *crema*, in bread was the basis of binding together.

The Italian news reports quite a few stories about food, explaining dishes made in restaurants from north to south, and offering spectacular presentations on feast days and holidays: the turbot polka-dotted in capers, the lamb with a pear in its mouth. More frequently than charts of calories or scientific messages about the latest food fad, there will be features on tradition and waste. Some weeks ago, people were interviewed outside grocery stores to find out how much of the bread they bought each day was thrown away. When the numbers added up to 25 percent, a campaign began. It was not about eating less bread for reasons of losing weight, but about not wasting a product too important to treat in any other way than as if it were life itself.

When a school lunch program had to be supplemented by parents paying a bill, the children whose parents didn't pay were refused the hot meal. The uproar reached the national news. Cultural tempers rose. Public opinion mounted: It was unfair to humiliate children because of their parents and not allow them to eat what the others had. The school grudgingly offered each a roll and a bottle of water. The public fury rose higher. In the end, a benefactor, who remembered, he said, what it was like not to eat and what it was like to be singled out, undertook the subscription of the children's lunches and lifted them into a collective sense of class equality.

2

The snail, the symbol of the Slow Food movement, unfolds perfectly what keeping to one's roots reflects. Going at a slow pace is part of the emphasis on destination. The race is about carrying forward the house, the shell, of what one is and knows. Every day is a good measure. Local is not boring; it is the way to really taste life. Founded in 1986, after a protest over whether a McDonald's restaurant would be installed near the Spanish Steps—the place where Bernini's fountain still dripped and tourists climbed the stairs to the rooms where John Keats died—the movement was shaped by Carlo Petrini, who slowly expanded its purpose to defending ecosystems and supporting organic methods. It was Virgil, the poet who chose to live in Ischia, near Naples, because life in Rome was too intense, who pointed out in the *Bucolics* that a civilization was in decline once citizens could no longer walk to the sources where the food they were eating was being produced. That's how new and old the idea of Slow Food is.

The movement has grown worldwide. But it is a beautiful thing to see that in Italy, although it is the basis of trendy restaurants, it is often a far quieter endeavor than that and remains a

practice off the tourist trails. It reflects conservative wisdom and skeptical views of profit and speed. It embraces commonsense approaches that have little to do with fads or exclusivity.

When our daughter was at university, she asked us to find a place to eat during the truffle season. All along the string of little villages and towns outside of our city, many seasonal food festivals are held. There are the grape and harvest festivals. There are the truffle meals offered in late October and early November. The atmosphere is seldom pretentious. Sometimes the meals are offered outdoors, with people sitting on benches among others who might be friends but probably are strangers. Whole pigs turn and crackle on spits, and squares of dough, fried in deep vats of oil, send out fragrant invitations. But the food, even at the most popular of festivals, is sophisticated and carefully composed in order to celebrate the element that has come into its own month.

The restaurant that we visited that foggy and rainy November night, climbing the mountain road in utter darkness, wondering why we were on this silly adventure, was a plain place, which we finally reached in a frightening downpour. We were there to eat; we were there because our daughter had wanted us to try truffles. She wanted us to be part of a local tradition. Why were we the only oddballs who failed to partake in this collective act? Everyone ate a truffle meal in November.

Fifteen years later, we still climb that mountain road, and often eat dishes that we have relished before. The menu is recited and, as if we were eating at home, we know there will still be the potato tortelli, and the four cakes we have eaten for years. There will be new dishes, chickpea soup with rosemary, trout with almonds, stuffed cabbage, or whatever else is in season. Truffles will return on cue. Each sausage comes with a story, each steak with a number and a provenance. It all might be overwhelming except that it is done without moralism or self-righteousness. It is done quietly, letting the food speak.

The wines are like rare books, in their complex tastes and in

their producers' testimonies to learning and experiment, to con-
servation and tradition. Work, that opening theme in the Italian
constitution, work, that curse and that respectable necessity, is
celebrated in the wines. The wines are what Italy does well, a joining of past and present, a building gutted and modernized but
keeping all its outer walls and that insistence on the past. Wines
that are alive and never the same. There are good years and bad
ones; the method counts, the method that accepts staying small
and keeping in scale with hands and feet and the sustainable
earth.

The restaurant has over thirty thousand bottles of wine,
which are served to truck drivers and salesmen, to farmers and professors. Here there is, as is true of so much in the country, a leveling
that occurs because one has a sense of belonging to tradition.
Drinking a good wine does not depend on having made a fortune
in the stock market, although that could be a reason. The costs are
not blinding. There is no aura created by Italian advertising that
implies depth and beauty are yours because of hard work and invest-
ments. The local people, shrewd about fair prices, are not fools.

The wines the owner brings out are often one of a kind. She
and her husband will have traveled throughout Italy, France, and
Croatia, listening to stories of fathers and sons, wives and hus-
bands using labor- and time-intensive technologies that have been
in the family for decades, sometimes centuries. The winemaking,
not always but often, consists in two or three thousand bottles of
a variety. The wine is a celebration of a year, all of its weather, its
conditions, its work. Its luminous amber color is for that meal,
that moment, a result of beliefs that are not always easy to hold or
easy to foresee as surviving in the future. Profit is a concept that
has limits. Taste is all. Ripeness is all. All is every moment centered on the vine's roots, the grapes' swelling, the particular abundant or scarce harvest.

The owner of the restaurant lives above it. Her parents, who
ran the restaurant when it offered only local rough red wine, still

keep their hands in. The mother, still beautiful in her late seventies and bent over from decades of labor and osteoporosis, continues to pay her contributions for her state pension. She likes to feel that she remains on the workers' side.

The snail is far from what one thinks of when Italy seems best characterized by Ferraris, palaces, and scandal-plagued politicians. It is the antithesis of the terrifying violence and ruin brought about by the Mafia and by corruption. The snail, which Primo Levi wrote about as "gracious repulsive logarithmic," is an interesting place to stop. "Why run," he asks the snail, "when it's enough to close yourself up to have peace?"

Here is the whole poem:

THE SNAIL

Why hurry, when you are well protected?
Is one place better than another
Once it has moisture and grass?
Why run, and run the risk of adventure,
When it's enough to close yourself up to have peace?
And then, if the universe becomes your enemy
You know how to seal yourself silently
Behind your veil of thin calcium
And negate the world and yourself in it.
But when the field is soaked with dew
Or rain has softened the soil
Every journey is a highway
Paved by your beautiful shiny secretions
Bridge from leaf to leaf and from stone to stone.
Navigating cautiously secure and secret,
With telescopic eyes you try
Gracious repugnant logarithmic.
Here you find a he-she partner
And taste trepidly

Tense and pulsing outside the shell
Timid enchantments of uncertain love.

(Translated by Wallis Wilde-Menozzi)

3

The snail is not the first image that comes to mind for a country synonymous with discovery and innovation. It hardly illuminates the creativity of Antonioni, or Pinafarina, or Benetton, or Renzo Piano, or Renata Tebaldi, or whomever else you may wish to pause with: Petrarch, Michelangelo, Lavinia Fontana, Cicero, Christopher Columbus, Vivaldi, Verdi, Marconi. But it snags the imagination and has resonance. The snail hardly calls up the image of Italian drivers, or soldiers, or philosophers like Machiavelli, or educators like Maria Montessori, or scientists like Enrico Fermi, or engineers who built so many of the highways of North Africa and the bridges of South America, or actresses like Anna Magnani, or tenors like Caruso. The snail, which curls in on itself, is surprising to link to this old country of fiery passions. Yet in the snail there

is a steady pace, a form that reflects life and death, a spiral that heralds perfect beauty without beginning and end.

In the millions of years contained in marble we see the snail and all the crustaceans, the shrimplike forms, the ammonites, fossils that were once under the sea and got tossed up into the pink mountains of the Dolomites. We see accretion. We see Vico's spiral of civil life narrated philosophically: why the straight line cannot proceed through the torturous twists of human life. Put the snail up against the mountain and take in its mystery. It is not a bad image for the solidity, the lack of upset and resistance over a model that does not see progress as simply measured and measured by the individual.

The snail cannot and will not travel like a bird or a gazelle. It pauses, and the shell that is such a defining feature suggests a life that can bear staying in place. The snail eats everything green and tender in the garden, but he is like the piazzas, with his shape like fixed stone. He progresses in a sublime form that suggests eternity. The shell is a coiled sign of beauty, containing, from the beginning, a sense of limits and of home. The snail ultimately has an exit strategy and leaves an empty space that can immediately be identified as having belonged to a living creature that always knew that having a home was important.

Italy has that steady pace that belies much of its surface commotion. Italians have an immense amount of tolerance, patience, solidity, community spirit, and sophisticated knowledge that works in the everyday in spite of all that might seem to run counter to that. Underneath the cautious view, the long view, the cynical view, the anarchical view, the extreme individualism, is the view that only a few things really matter. That robust steadiness counts on the truth of interconnectedness and the satisfactions offered by having a base and a basis for things.

ACKNOWLEDGMENTS

When she pointed out how happy I was during a short family vacation spent in Rome a few years ago, my daughter, unknowingly, announced this book to me. The unmistakable flame of a project posed its flickering heat while we visited old haunts. Once again, the Eternal City would show me my fate.

A wonderful rush of memories started moving as I looked again at the years in which I lived in Rome. Many of my early experiences emerged as subjects, in large part because the physical core of the city remained as a way of confirming them. But decades of time had passed. Bridging the years with a voice that could carry both my past and the present was far more complicated than it seemed. As I looked back, issues of perspective became central, revealing that there was no single connecting path for speech except for the one I had found in Rome the first time: the ancient river. The voice that carried me through these pages was never meant to be the voice of a scholar or expository journalist. It was one gathered from memory, personal feeling, and facts that might suggest how each of us subjectively makes the world her own.

I could not have written this book without the help of many people. For years, Jonathan Galassi has held out an encouraging hand. His sensibility and human touch have strengthened my work and offered me a place in the crucial dialogue among cross-cultural writers. I am grateful to him for this. Miranda Popkey liberated my manuscript by using her great intelligence and meticulousness. It was inspiring to work with her.

Many people read the manuscript early on, including my brother Alex Wilde; my sister, Lisa Wilde; my friends Susan Tiberghien, Elizabeth Pauncz, Maria Laurino, and Kathy Cambor; and my agent, Susan Schulman. Rab Hatfield brought decades of experience as an art historian in Italy to parts of the final manuscript. My husband, Paolo Menozzi, always adds perspective to my Italian work. He read this book several times, while carrying more than his share of daily duties and putting up with the intense focus that book-writing requires. To all of them, thanks for their loving participation. My gratitude also extends to Simona Rizzo in Parma, who prepared all the image files with skill and good humor. To the many talented people at Farrar, Straus and Giroux who saw a book with lots of photographic detail through production, I thank them for their patience in dealing with its complexities.

As I tried to delineate the period of breakup following my father's death, I was brought very close to the solidity that remains, even today, from the way my siblings and I were raised. We were given a great deal, including one another. Memories of my growing up in Wisconsin, along with questions about the sacrifices in my parents' lost dreams, are deep parts of my self. The book, while never conceived as a memoir, is dedicated to my early family.

As the book took shape, photos became another line for suggesting thoughts and patterns. It was Jonathan Galassi who encouraged me to include them. I was given the chance to photograph Michelangelo's unfinished *Prisoners* in the Accademia in Florence when the museum was closed, even to professionals. The official, after listening to my request, made an exception. "But I can let you do this only if you use a simple noncommercial pocket camera. No tripod, lights, flash, ladders." Once again, I was the benefactress of Italian flexibility. I would be alone with Michelangelo.

I rang a bell at a side door to the museum at the appointed hour and an assistant handed me my permit. At the end of the corridor loomed what may well be the most famous statue in the world. I didn't think for a moment to take any shots of the *David*, since I had agreed to photograph only the *Prisoners* and *Saint Matthew*. After about an hour of deep attention, I began to experience sounds. Was this a variation of the Stendhal syndrome, when people got dizzy and fainted, overwhelmed by art? Security video cameras and air temperature controls might well have been emitting sounds that normally crowd noises would cover. However, I was still captivated by extremely soft, distant vibrations. The sensation grew: All surfaces were imperceptibly trembling. While it would be impossible to prove, I believe that I saw the world Michelangelo saw. It was our world—one halfway toward another.

ILLUSTRATION CREDITS

I would like to thank the individuals and institutions listed below for their kind permission to reproduce the images in this book.

Whenever the term *Courtyard Musicians* appears in a credit, it refers to the musicians who practiced in the cellar underneath Rosina's room when I lived in the Arco degli Acetari. For one of my birthdays, they presented me with a photo album of the people in the courtyard, taken on a day when the local priest was celebrating a Mass there and blessing their houses. Thus the windows are festooned with bedspreads and tablecloths to add to the look of ritual majesty. They signed the book—Alessio, Renato, Maurizio, Antonio, Riccardo. The gift captured, then and even more now, the shared atmosphere of that place.

119 Ministry of Pardon and Justice, Rome: WWM

123, 125 Bologna train station: WWM

127 Correggio, *L'Assunzione della Vergine*, Duomo, Parma: Franco Furoncoli

131 Correggio, detail of Mary in *L'Assunzione della Vergine*, Duomo, Parma: Franco Furoncoli

133 Correggio, detail of *L'Assunzione della Vergine*, Duomo, Parma: Franco Furoncoli

135 Rosina, courtyard: Courtyard Musicians / Author's Collection

141 Detail of the Capitoline Wolf, Museo Nuovo, Palazzo dei Conservatori, Rome: WWM with the permission of Roma, Musei Capitolini

143 Newspaper stand: WWM

146 The author buying the paper in Rome: Author's Collection

149 The jockey Trecciolino rounding the San Martino curve, Piazza del Campo, Siena: Roberto Vicario / Creative Commons

155 Detail of the Gaia Fountain, Piazza del Campo, Siena: WWM

156 Piazza del Campo, Siena: WWM

166 Duccio, *Maestà*, Museo dell'Opera Metropolitana, Siena: Nimatallah / Art Resource, NY

167 *Minerva*, Roman statue, Museo Nazionale Romano, Palazzo Massimo alle Terme, Rome: WWM with the permission of Ministero per i Beni e le Attività Culturali, Roma—Soprintendenza Speciale per i Beni Archeologici di Roma

169 Duccio, detail of *Maestà*, Museo dell'Opera Metropolitana, Siena: WWM with the permission of Ministero per i Beni e le Attività Culturali—Soprintendenza per i Beni Storici, Artistici ed Etnoantropologici per le Province di Siena e Grosseto

171 Ambrogio Lorenzetti, detail of *The Blessings of Good Government*, Palazzo Pubblico, Siena: Erich Lessing / Art Resource, NY

175 San Pietrini, Rome: WWM

180 (*top*) San Pietrini, Parma: WWM

180 (*bottom*) San Pietrini, Rome: WWM

183 Plaster cast of a victim of the eruption of Mount Vesuvius in C.E., 79 Pompeii: WWM

187 Jean-Baptiste Chapuy, after Alessandro d'Anna, *The Eruption of Mount Etna in 1766*: Print Collection, Miriam and Ira D. Wallach Division of Art, Prints and Photographs, The New York Public Library, Astor, Lenox and Tilden Foundations

191 Detail of a mosaic, Pompeii: WWM

193 Temple of Hera, Metaponto: WWM

196 Roman bust, Metaponto Museum, Metaponto: WWM with the permission of Ministero per i Beni e le Attività Culturali—Direzione Regionale per i Beni Culturali e Paesaggistici della Basilicata—Soprintendenza per i Beni Archeologici della Basilicata

PERMISSIONS ACKNOWLEDGMENTS

Printed in the USA
CPSIA information can be obtained
at www.ICGtesting.com
LVHW040904150724
785511LV00003B/287